P9-AOS-715

THE BEST OF **ИНОСТРАНКА**

ALESSANDRO BARICCO

Seta

АЛЕССАНДРО БАРИККО

Шёлк

Роман

Перевод с итальянского

Геннадия Киселева

Издательство "Иностранка"

Москва, 2005

УДК 821.131.1–3Барикко
ББК 84(4Ита)–44
   Б25

*Художественное оформление
и макет* А.Бондаренко

Барикко А.

Б25   Шёлк: Роман / Пер. с итал. Г.Киселева. – М.: Иностранка: 2005. – 151 с. – (The best of Иностранка).

ISBN 5–94145–295–0

Роман А.Барикко «Шёлк» — один из самых ярких
итальянских бестселлеров конца XX века. Место
действия романа — Япония. Время действия — конец XIX века. Так что никаких самолетов, стираль-
ных машин и психоанализа, предупреждает нас ав-
тор. Об этом как-нибудь в другой раз. А пока —
пленившая Европу и Америку, тонкая как шелк по-
весть о женщине-призраке и неудержимой страсти.

УДК 821.131–3Барикко
ББК 84(4Ита)–44

ISBN 5–94145–295–0

© 1966 R.C.S. Libri and Grandi Opere S.p.A, Milano
© Г.Киселев, перевод на русский язык, 1999
© "Иностранка", оформление, 2004
© "Иностранка", издание на русском языке, 2005

1

Хотя отец и рисовал для него блестящую карьеру военного, в конечном счете Эрве Жонкур стал зарабатывать себе на жизнь весьма необычным ремеслом, которому, по иронии судьбы, была не чужда особенность настолько привлекательная, что выдавала смутную *женскую* интонацию.

Эрве Жонкур зарабатывал на жизнь тем, что покупал и продавал шелковичных червей.

Шел 1861. Флобер сочинял "Саламбо", электрическое освещение значилось в догадках, а по ту сторону Океана Авраам Линкольн вел войну, конца которой он так и не увидит.

[6]   Эрве Жонкуру было 32 года.
Он покупал и продавал.
Шелковичных червей.

2

Вернее сказать, Эрве Жонкур покупал и продавал шелковичных червей, когда они пребывали еще не в виде червей, а в виде крошечных желтовато-серых яичек, неподвижных и как будто мертвых. На одной ладони их помещалось видимо-невидимо.

"Все равно что держать в руке целое состояние".

В начале мая яйца раскрывались, высвобождая личинку. Через месяц лихорадочного поедания тутовых листьев личинка окуклялась, навивая кокон. А еще через две недели окончательно прободала его, оставляя по себе солидный прибыток, выражавшийся в тысяче метров грубой шелковой

[8] нити и кругленькой сумме французских франков. При условии, что все проходило строго по правилам и — как в случае с Эрве Жонкуром — в каком-нибудь подходящем местечке на юге Франции.

Лавильдье — так звалось местечко, где жил Эрве Жонкур.

Элен — так звали его жену.

Детей у них не было.

3

Дабы избежать пагубных последствий мора, то и дело опустошавшего европейские рассадники, Эрве Жонкур все больше склонялся к покупке яиц шелкопряда за Средиземным морем, в Сирии и Египте. В этом заключалась утонченно-рискованная сторона его ремесла. Что ни год, в первых числах января он отправлялся в путь. Тысяча шестьсот миль по морю и восемьсот верст по суше. Он отбирал товар, приценивался и покупал. Затем проделывал обратный путь — восемьсот верст по суше, тысяча шестьсот миль по морю — и поспевал в Лавильдье как раз в первое воскресенье апреля. Как раз к Праздничной мессе.

[10] Еще две недели уходили на то, чтобы разложить и продать кладки яиц.

Остаток года он отдыхал.

4

— Какая она, Африка? — спрашивали его.

— Усталая.

У него был большой дом прямо за окраиной городка и маленькая мастерская в центре — прямо напротив заброшенного дома Жана Бербека.

Однажды Жан Бербек решил, что не будет больше говорить. И сдержал слово. Жена и двое дочерей ушли от него. Он умер. На дом никто не позарился, вот и стоял он в полном запустении.

Покупая и продавая шелковичных червей, Эрве Жонкур зарабатывал достаточно, чтобы обеспечить себе и своей жене те удобства, которые в провинции принято

[12] считать роскошью. Он умело заправлял хозяйством, во всем знал меру, ну а вероятность — вполне достижимая — по-настоящему разбогатеть оставляла его совершенно равнодушным. Тем более что был он из тех, кому по душе *созерцать* собственную жизнь и кто не приемлет всякий соблазн *участвовать* в ней.

Замечено, что такие люди наблюдают за своей судьбой примерно так, как большинство людей за дождливым днем.

5

Спроси его кто-нибудь, Эрве Жонкур ответил бы, что готов жить так вечно. Но вот, в начале шестидесятых, моровое поветрие пебрины напрочь загубило рассадники шелкопряда в Европе, пахнув к тому же за море, в Африку, а по слухам, и в Индию. Когда в 1861 Эрве Жонкур вернулся из очередного путешествия со свежей кладкой яиц, спустя два месяца почти весь выводок был охвачен недугом. Для Лавильдье, как и для множества других мест, благоденствие которых держалось на шелковом деле, тот год показался началом конца. Наука была бессильна разгадать причины мора. Весь белый свет, до крайних своих

[14] пределов, находился точно в плену у зага-
дочного колдовства.

— Весь, *да не весь*, — тихо молвил Бальдабью. — Да не весь, — добавил он, разбавляя
на два пальца свой перно.

6

Бальдабью был тем самым человеком, который появился в здешних краях двадцать лет назад, прямиком направился к городскому голове, без объявлений вломился в его кабинет, раскинул на столе шелковый шарф цвета вечерней зари и спросил:

— Как по-вашему, что это?

— Женские фитюльки.

— Не угадали. Фитюльки, только мужские: звонкая монета.

Городской голова велел выставить его за дверь. Тогда Бальдабью построил вниз по реке прядильню, на опушке леса — ригу для разведения шелкопряда, а на развилке вивьерской дороги — часовенку в честь святой Агнессы. Нанял десятка три работников, выписал из Италии диковинную деревянную машину — сплошные шестеренки да колесики — и не изрек ни слова еще семь месяцев. Потом снова нагрянул к городскому голове и выложил на стол тридцать тысяч франков крупными купюрами в аккуратных стопках.

— Как по-вашему, что это?

— Звонкая монета.

— Не угадали. Это доказательство того, что вы олух царя небесного.

Бальдабью собрал деньги, запихнул их в суму и пошел к выходу.

Городской голова остановил его:

— Что от меня требуется, черт подери?

— Ничего — и вы станете самым богатым городским головой в округе.

Через пять лет в Лавильдье было семь прядилен; городок стал одним из главных шелководческих и ткацких центров Европы. Бальдабью не был его единственным владельцем. На этом необычном поприще он обрел последователей среди местной знати и помещиков. Каждому из них Бальдабью без утайки раскрывал секреты ремесла. Это занимало его куда больше, чем тривиальное огребание денег лопатой. Он наставлял. И щедро делился тайнами. Такой он был человек.

7

А еще Бальдабью был именно тем человеком, который восемь лет назад изменил жизнь Эрве Жонкура. В то время первые моровые пагубы уже начали изводить европейские плантации шелкопряда. Бальдабью хладнокровно обмозговал положение и пришел к выводу, что задачу не нужно решать, ее нужно обойти. План у него созрел, не хватало только исполнителя. Он понял, что нашел его, когда впервые увидел Эрве Жонкура. Тот проходил мимо кабачка Вердена в щегольском мундире пехотного подпоручика, горделиво вышагивая, как и подобает молодому офицеру в отпуске. Тогда ему минуло 24. Бальдабью зазвал его к себе, развернул перед ним атлас, пестревший экзотическими названиями, и сказал:

— Поздравляю, мой мальчик. Ты наконец-то нашел серьезную работу.

Эрве Жонкур выслушал причудливый рассказ о шелкопрядах, личинках, пирамидах и морских странствиях. А потом сказал:

— Я не могу.

— Что так?

— Через два дня у меня кончается отпуск. Я должен вернуться в Париж.

— Военная карьера?

— Да. Такова воля отца.

— Это не вопрос.

И он повел Эрве Жонкура к отцу.

— Как по-вашему, кто это? — спросил Бальдабью, без объявлений вломившись в кабинет отца.

— Мой сын.

— Взгляните получше.

Городской голова откинулся на спинку кожаного кресла и почувствовал, что потеет.

— Это мой сын Эрве Жонкур. Через два дня он вернется в Париж. Там его ждет блестящая карьера в нашей доблестной армии, если на то будет воля Господа и святой Агнессы.

— Верно. Только у Господа и других дел по горло, а святая Агнесса терпеть не может военных.

Через месяц Эрве Жонкур отправился в Египет. Он вышел в море на корабле под названием "Адель". В каютах витали ароматы камбуза, некий англичанин уверял, что бился при Ватерлоо, вечером третьего дня на горизонте, словно хмельные волны, блеснули дельфины, в рулетку без конца выпадало шестнадцать.

Вернулся он спустя два месяца — в первое воскресенье апреля, как раз к Праздничной мессе — с двумя деревянными кофрами: проложенные ватой, там почивали тысячи яичек шелкопряда. В придачу у него накопилась уйма всевозможных историй. Но когда они остались наедине, Бальдабью спросил его лишь об одном:

— Расскажи мне о дельфинах.

— О дельфинах?

— О том, когда ты их видел.

Таким был этот Бальдабью.

Никто не знал, сколько ему лет.

8

— Весь, *да не весь*, — тихо молвил Бальдабью. — Да не весь, — добавил он, разбавляя
на два пальца свой перно.

Август, время за полночь. Обычно в этот
час кабачок Вердена давно уже закрывал-
ся. Перевернутые стулья рядком выстраи-
вались на столах. Стойка и все прочее были
отчищены. Оставалось погасить свет и за-
крыть кабачок. Но Верден терпеливо ждал.
Бальдабью продолжал говорить.

Эрве Жонкур сидел напротив с потухшей
сигаретой во рту и неподвижно слушал. Как
и восемь лет назад, он безропотно позво-
лял этому человеку заново выстраивать его
судьбу. Тихая, отчетливая речь перемежа-

лась ритмичными глотками перно. Бальдабью не смолкал в течение долгих минут.
А напоследок заключил:

— У нас нет выбора. Если мы хотим вы-
жить, нам нужно дотуда добраться.

Молчание.

Облокотившись о стойку, Верден поднял
на них глаза.

Бальдабью целиком отдался поискам
лишнего глотка перно со дна стакана.

Эрве Жонкур примостил сигарету на
краю стола, прежде чем сказать:

— А вообще, где она, эта Япония?

Бальдабью поднял палку, направив ее по-
верх церкви Святого Огюста.

— Прямо, не сворачивая.

Сказал он.

— И так до самого конца света.

9

В те времена Япония и впрямь была на другом конце света. Два столетия остров, собранный из островов, существовал в полном отрыве от остального мира, пренебрегая всякой связью с континентом, не подпуская к себе иноземцев. Китайский берег отстоял миль на двести, но императорский указ способствовал тому, чтобы он откатился еще дальше: указом повсеместно запрещалось строительство двух- или трехмачтовых кораблей. Следуя по-своему дальновидной логике, указ не возбранял покидать родину, зато обрекал на смерть каждого, кто посмеет вернуться. Китайские, голландские и английские купцы не раз пытались прорвать эту нелепую обособленность, но им всего-навсего удавалось сплести непрочную и чреватую опасностями сеть контрабанды. В итоге они довольствовались мизерным барышом, кучей неприятностей и расхожими байками, которые травили по вечерам в каком-нибудь порту. Там, где оплошали купцы, преуспели, бряцая оружием, американцы. В июле 1853 коммодор Мэтью К. Перри вошел в бухту Иокогамы с новейшей флотилией паровых судов и предъявил японцам ультиматум, в коем "уповалось" на доступность острова для иностранцев.

До этого японцы видом не видывали, чтобы морской корабль шел против ветра.

Когда семь месяцев спустя Перри вернулся за ответом на свой ультиматум, военное правительство острова пошло на подписание договора, по которому чужакам разрешался доступ в два северных порта Страны. Сверх того, им дозволялось заключать первые, весьма умеренные сделки. "Отныне море, омывающее этот остров, — объявил с некоторой помпезностью коммодор, — станет гораздо мельче".

Обо всем этом Бальдабью прекрасно знал. Знал он и о легенде, которая не сходила с языка у побывавших там странников. Легенда гласила, что на острове выделывают шелк, какого на всем белом свете не сыскать. Выделывают добрую тысячу лет таинственным способом, достигшим чудесного совершенства. И все бы хорошо, только Бальдабью полагал, что никакая это не легенда, а самая настоящая правда. Однажды он держал в руках платок, вытканный из шелковой японской нити. Так держат в руках воздух. И когда все, казалось, пошло прахом из-за кутерьмы с пебриной и недужными червями, он разом смекнул:

— Стоит себе остров. Шелкопряда на нем хоть отбавляй. И коли за двести лет на этот остров не ступила нога китайского купчишки или аглицкого страховщика, то никакой заразе туда вовек не дойти.

И не просто смекнул, а известил всех местных шелкоделов, собрав их в кабачке Вердена. Никто из них отродясь ни слыхивал ни о какой Японии.

— Это что же нам, за отборными кладками теперь полсвета отмахать прикажешь? И куда? У них как завидят чужака, так мигом его и вздернут.

— Вздергивали, — поправил Бальдабью.

Шелкоделы не знали, что и думать. Кое-кто возражал:

— Почему же никому до сих пор не пришло в голову закупать там кладки?

Бальдабью мог бы для порядка и приврать, напомнив честному народу, что другого такого Бальдабью им днем с огнем не найти. Но он предпочел выложить все начистоту:

— Японцы смирились с тем, что шелк придется продавать. Но не кладки яиц. Их они берегут как зеницу ока. И объявляют преступником всякого, кто осмелится вывезти кладки с острова.

Шелководы из Лавильдье в большинстве своем были людьми добропорядочными. Им и в голову бы не пришло нарушать закон в собственной стране. Зато перспектива сделать это на другом конце света, похоже, устраивала их вполне.

11

Шел 1861. Флобер заканчивал "Саламбо", электрическое освещение значилось в числе догадок, а по ту сторону Океана Авраам Линкольн вел войну, конца которой он так и не увидит. Шелководы из Лавильдье объединились в товарищество и собрали порядочную сумму, необходимую для проведения экспедиции. Они сочли разумным доверить ее Эрве Жонкуру. Когда Бальдабью спросил его согласия, в ответ он услышал вопрос:

— А все-таки, где она, эта Япония?

Прямо, не сворачивая. И так до самого конца света.

Он двинулся в путь 6 октября. Один.

На окраине Лавильдье он обнял Элен и [29]
проронил:

— Ты не должна ничего бояться.

Она была высокой и медлительной. У нее были длинные темные волосы, которые она никогда не собирала в пучок. И чарующий голос.

Эрве Жонкур двинулся в путь, имея при себе восемьдесят тысяч франков золотом и полученные от Бальдабью имена трех людей: китайца, голландца и японца. Он пересек границу возле Меца, проехал Вюртемберг и Баварию, въехал в Австрию, поездом добрался до Вены и Будапешта, а затем напрямую до Киева. Отмахал на перекладных две тысячи верст по русской равнине, перевалил через Уральский хребет, углубился в просторы Сибири, сорок дней колесил по ней до озера Байкал, которое в тех краях называют "морем". Прошел Амур вниз по течению вдоль китайской границы до самого Океана. Дойдя до

Океана, просидел в порту Сабирк одиннадцать дней, покуда корабль голландских контрабандистов не доставил его до мыса Тэрая на западном побережье Японии. Окольными путями пересек префектуры Исикава, Тояма и Ниигата, вступил в провинцию Фукусима, дошел до города Сиракава, обогнул его с восточной стороны, двое суток дожидался человека в черном, который завязал ему глаза и провел в деревню на холмах, где он заночевал, а наутро сторговал партию яиц шелкопряда у бессловесного человека, чье лицо скрывал шелковый платок. На закате он укрыл товар в своей поклаже, встал к Японии спиной и тронулся в обратный путь.

Не успел Эрве Жонкур выйти за околицу, как его догнал и остановил какой-то селянин. Он что-то возбужденно затараторил и с любезной решительностью повел чужестранца назад.

Эрве Жонкур не знал по-японски и потому не уяснил речей селянина. Но понял, что Хара Кэй хочет его видеть.

13

Перегородка из рисовой бумаги отъехала вбок, и Эрве Жонкур вошел. На полу, в самом дальнем углу комнаты, скрестив ноги, сидел Хара Кэй. Темная туника, никаких украшений. Единственная зримая примета власти — недвижно лежащая рядом женщина: голова покоится на его животе, глаза сомкнуты, руки скрыты в широком алом кимоно, полыхающем как пламя на пепельной циновке. Он медленно запускает пальцы в ее волосы, словно поглаживая шерстку задремавшего ценного зверька.

Эрве Жонкур пересек комнату, подождал, пока хозяин сделает ему знак, и сел напротив. Какое-то время они молчали, глядя друг другу в глаза. Из ниоткуда возник слуга, поставил перед ними две чашки чая и вновь обратился в ничто. Хара Кэй заговорил на своем языке. Его напевный голос истончался в назойливо-искусственном фальцете. Эрве Жонкур слушал. Он не отрывал глаз от глаз Хара Кэя и лишь на миг, почти непроизвольно, опустил их на женское лицо.

Это было лицо девочки.

Он поднял глаза.

Хара Кэй прервался, взял одну из чашек, поднес ее к губам и, помедлив, произнес:

— Попробуйте рассказать о себе.

Он произнес это по-французски, слегка растягивая гласные, хрипловатым, искренним голосом.

Недоступнейшему из японцев, хозяину всего, что пришельцам удавалось вывезти с чуждедальнего острова, попытался Эрве Жонкур рассказать, кто он такой. Он говорил на родном языке, говорил не торопясь, даже не зная наверное, способен ли Хара Кэй понять его. Словно по наитию отбросил он излишние опасения и без прикрас и умолчаний поведал всю правду. Просто и ясно. Монотонным голосом и скупыми жестами он выстраивал в общий ряд незначительные подробности и главные события, подражая гипнотическому порядку меланхолично-сухой описи уцелевших после пожара вещей. Хара Кэй слушал — черт его лица не тронул и слабый налет выразительности. Он сосредоточенно смотрел на губы Эрве Жонкура, точно это были последние строки прощального письма. В комнате царили такая тишина и неподвижность, что происшедшее вдруг, при всей своей ничтожности, показалось чем-то неимоверным.

Внезапно,
без малейшего движения,
лежащая девушка
открыла глаза.

Не прерываясь, Эрве Жонкур бессознательно устремил на нее взгляд, и вот что он увидел, по-прежнему не обрывая речи: у этих глаз *не было восточного разреза*; и еще: они взирали на него *с пронзительной остротой*, как будто с самого начала неустанно следили за ним из-под век. Эрве Жонкур отвел взгляд со всей непринужденностью, на какую был способен, стараясь продолжить рассказ и не допустить излишнего перепада в голосе. Он прервался, лишь когда его взгляд упал на чашку чая, стоявшую перед ним на полу. Взял ее одной рукой, поднес к губам, отпил маленький глоток. И снова заговорил, ставя чашку на прежнее место.

Франция, хождения за море, дух шелковицы из Лавильдье, поезда на паровой тяге, голос Элен. Эрве Жонкур продолжал рассказывать о своей жизни, чего еще не делал никогда в жизни. Девушка продолжала смотреть на него; ее неистовый взгляд властно принуждал всякое его слово звучать с особой значимостью. Когда вся комната сползла в полную неподвижность, из ее кимоно неожиданно выпросталась рука и бесшумно скользнула по циновке. Эрве Жонкур видел, как это бледное пятно дотянулось до границы его зрительного поля, коснулось чашки Хара Кэя, а затем, необъяснимым образом, заскользило дальше, до следующей чашки — той самой, из которой неотвратимо пил *он сам*, — без колебаний взялось за нее, легонько вздело и унесло с собой. Хара Кэй ни на секунду не отвлекался от невозмутимого созерцания губ Эрве Жонкура.

Девушка чуть приподняла голову.

Впервые отвела она взгляд от Эрве Жонкура и направила его на чашку.

Медленно повернула чашку, пока губы в точности не совпали с тем местом, где пил он.

Прищурив глаза, сделала глоток.

Отстранила чашку от губ.

Спрятала руку в складках одежды.

Склонила голову на живот Хара Кэя.

Пристально глядя в глаза Эрве Жонкура.

Эрве Жонкур говорил еще долго. Он примолк, лишь когда Хара Кэй отвел от него взгляд и еле заметно кивнул.

Молчание.

Слегка растягивая гласные, хрипловатым, искренним голосом Хара Кэй произнес по-французски:

— Надумаете вернуться — приятно будет вас видеть.

Впервые он улыбнулся.

— Вместо яичек шелкопряда вам подсунули рыбью икру: грош ей цена.

Эрве Жонкур потупился. Перед ним стояла чашка чая. Он взял ее и, вращая, начал осматривать, словно выискивал что-то на цветной каемке. Найдя, что искал, он пригубил чашку и выпил ее до дна. Затем поставил чашку перед собой и сказал:

— Я знаю.

Хара Кэй весело засмеялся.

— Оттого-то и расплатились фальшивым золотом?

— По товару и монета.

Хара Кэй посерьезнел.

— Вы получите то, за чем пришли, когда покинете эти места.

— А вы получите ваше золото, когда я покину этот остров целым и невредимым. Вот вам мое слово.

Эрве Жонкур не стал дожидаться ответа. Он поднялся, отступил назад и поклонился.

Напоследок он увидел ее глаза: совершенно безмолвные, они неотрывно смотрели в его глаза.

17

Через шесть дней Эрве Жонкур сел в Такао-ке на корабль голландских контрабандистов, доставивший его в Сабирк. Оттуда, вдоль китайской границы, он поднялся до озера Байкал, проделал четыре тысячи верст по сибирским просторам, перевалил через Уральский хребет, добрался до Киева, поездом проехал всю Европу с востока на запад и после трехмесячного путешествия прибыл во Францию. В первое воскресенье апреля — как раз к Праздничной мессе — он показался у въезда в Лавильдье. Остановился, возблагодарил Господа и вступил в город, считая шаги, чтобы у каждого шага было свое имя и чтобы уже не забыть их никогда.

— Ну и какой он, конец света? — спросил у него Бальдабью.

— Невидимый.

В подарок жене он привез шелковую тунику, которую стеснительная Элен так ни разу и не надела. Возьмешь ее в руки — и кажется, держишь в руках воздух.

Яичные кладки, привезенные Эрве Жонкуром из Японии, оказались вполне здоровы-
ми, после того как их высадили на множество
мелко нарезанных листьев тутового дерева.
Шелк в округе Лавильдье выдался в тот год
каких свет не видал: и количеством и доб-
ротностью. Решили открыть еще две прядильни, а Бальдабью соорудил клуатр возле
часовенки Святой Агнессы. Он почему-то во-
образил его круглым и заказал проект испан-
скому архитектору Хуану Бенитесу, постро-
ившему немало арен для боя быков.

— Да, и никакого песка: посредине мы ра-
зобьем сквер. И, если можно, у входа вместо бычьих голов — дельфиньи.

— Дельфиньи, сеньор?

— Ты рыбу когда-нибудь видел, Бенитес?

Эрве Жонкур подбил кое-какие счета и обнаружил, что богат. Он прикупил тридцать акров земли к югу от своих владений и все лето занимался разметкой парка для усладительных прогулок в тиши и спокойствии. Парк представлялся ему невидимым, как тот конец света. По утрам он хаживал к Вердену, где узнавал о местных новостях и просматривал газеты, доставленные из Парижа. Вечерами допоздна засиживался вместе с Элен на открытой веранде своего дома. Она читала вслух, и он чувствовал себя счастливым, думая про себя, что на всем белом свете нет голоса краше, чем ее голос.

4 сентября 1862 ему исполнилось 33 года. Жизнь струилась перед его взором как дождь: легко и безмятежно.

— Ты не должна ничего бояться.

Раз уж так решил Бальдабью, Эрве Жонкур снова отправился в Японию в первый день октября. Он пересек границу возле Меца, проехал Вюртемберг и Баварию, въехал в Австрию, поездом добрался до Вены и Будапешта, а затем напрямую до Киева. Отмахал на перекладных две тысячи верст по русской равнине, перевалил через Уральский хребет, углубился в просторы Сибири, сорок дней колесил по ней до озера Байкал, которое в тех краях называют "окаянным". Прошел Амур вниз по течению вдоль китайской границы до самого Океана. Дойдя до Океана, просидел в порту Сабирк одиннадцать дней, покуда корабль голландских контрабандистов не доставил его до мыса Тэрая на западном побережье Японии. Окольными путями миновал префектуры Исикава, Тояма и Ниигата, вступил в провинцию Фукусима, дошел до города Сиракава, обогнул его с восточной стороны, двое суток дожидался человека в черном, который завязал ему глаза и провел в деревню Хара Кэя. Когда он открыл глаза, перед ним стояли двое слуг. Они взяли его вещи и довели до опушки леса. Там они указали ему на тропинку и оставили чужеземца одного. Эрве Жонкур зашагал в тени, отхваченной у дневного света наседавшими со всех сторон деревьями. Он остановился, когда зеленая завеса на обочине вдруг на мгновение приоткрылась, словно окно. Метрах в тридцати книзу виднелось озеро. На берегу, спиной к нему, сидел Хара Кэй, а рядом — женщина в оранжевом платье, с распущенными по плечам волосами. Стоило Эрве Жонкуру взглянуть на нее, как она медленно повернулась, ровно на то короткое время, которого хватило, чтобы поймать его взгляд.

[46]   У ее глаз не было восточного разреза; ее лицо было лицом девочки.

Эрве Жонкур продолжил путь в чаще леса и, выйдя, очутился на самой кромке суши. Чуть впереди, на корточках сидел одетый в черное Хара Кэй. Сидел не двигаясь, один. Вблизи лежало сброшенное на землю оранжевое платье и пара соломенных сандалий. Эрве Жонкур подошел. Легкие покатые волны подгоняли озерную воду к берегу, будто присланные откуда-то издалека.

— Мой французский друг, — вымолвил Хара Кэй, не оборачиваясь.

Прошел не один час, пока они говорили и молчали, сидя друг подле друга. Затем Хара Кэй встал. Эрве Жонкур последовал за ним. Неуловимым движением, прежде чем ступить на тропинку, он выронил одну из своих перчаток рядом с оранжевым платьем, брошенным на берегу. В селение они пришли уже под вечер.

Эрве Жонкур гостил у Хара Кэя четыре дня. И жил как при дворе у короля. Все в том селении существовало ради этого человека; едва ли не каждое движение на окружных холмах свершалось, дабы охранить или ублажить его. Прочая жизнь кипела приглушенно, копошась украдкой, точно загнанный в логово зверь. Мир будто отдалился на века.

В распоряжении Эрве Жонкура был дом и пятеро слуг, сопровождавших его повсюду. Ел он один, под сенью цветущего дерева небывалой красоты. Дважды в день, с особой торжественностью, подавали чай. Вечером Эрве Жонкура приводили в просторную комнату с каменным полом, где совершался обряд омовения. Три пожилые женщины — на лицах подобие восковых масок — поливали водой и обтирали его тело теплой шелковой простыней. Руки у них были узловатые, а прикосновения — легкие.

Утром второго дня Эрве Жонкур наблюдал, как в селении появился белый человек. За ним катились две телеги, доверху груженные большими деревянными ящиками. Это был англичанин. Он приехал не покупать. Он приехал продавать.

— Оружие, месье. А вы?

— Я покупаю. Шелковичных червей.

Ужинали вместе. Англичанину было что рассказать. Восемь лет мерил он версты между Европой и Японией. Эрве Жонкур долго слушал, а под конец спросил:

— Не знакома ли вам молодая женщина, полагаю европейка, белая — что живет здесь?

Англичанин продолжал есть с непроницаемым видом.

— В Японии не бывает белых женщин. В Японии нет ни одной белой женщины.

На другой день он уехал с целой подводой золота.

Эрве Жонкур снова увидел Хара Кэя лишь утром третьего дня. Ни с того ни с сего пятеро его слуг, как по волшебству, улетучились, и через несколько мгновений возник он сам. Человек, ради которого вековали свой век здешние селяне, постоянно перемещался в неком пустом пузыре. Как будто негласный указ предписывал всему свету не нарушать его покоя.

Они взошли по косогору на отлогую поляну. Небо в вышине разлиновали десятки голубых большекрылых птиц.

— Местные жители смотрят на птиц и по их полету угадывают будущее.

Сказал Хара Кэй.

— Помню, в детстве отец привел меня на такую поляну, вложил в мои руки свой лук и велел стрелять по птицам. Я выстрелил, и голубая большекрылая птица камнем упала на землю. Угадай полет твоей стрелы, если хочешь знать, что ждет тебя впереди, сказал мне отец.

Птицы неторопливо парили в небе, то поднимаясь, то опускаясь, будто старательно пытались заштриховать его крыльями.

Они сошли в деревню при странном свете дня, казавшегося вечером. У дома Эрве Жонкура они распрощались. Хара Кэй повернулся и не спеша направился вниз по дорожке, сбегавшей вдоль реки. Эрве Жонкур задержался на пороге, глядя ему вслед. Он подождал, пока Хара Кэй отойдет шагов на двадцать, и произнес:

— Когда вы скажете мне, кто эта девушка?

Хара Кэй шел не останавливаясь, мерным шагом, в котором не было и тени усталости. Кругом царила полная тишина и опустошенность. Куда бы ни направлялся этот человек, он, словно по особому предписанию, погружался в совершенное и безграничное уединение.

Утром последнего дня Эрве Жонкур вышел побродить по деревне. Мужчины на его пути отвешивали поклоны; женщины, потупив взгляд, расплывались в улыбке. Он сообразил, что жилище Хара Кэя где-то рядом, когда разглядел громадную вольеру, вместившую немыслимое множество всеразличных птиц: чудеса, да и только. В разговоре с ним Хара Кэй признался, что выписывал их со всех концов света. Среди птиц были и такие, что стоили поболе всего шелка, который выткали бы в Лавильдье за год. Эрве Жонкур неподвижно смотрел на это великолепное безумие. Ему вспомнилась одна книга, в которой было сказано, что восточные мужчины, воздавая должное верности любимых женщин, имели обыкновение дарить им не драгоценности, но редких и восхитительных птиц.

Обитель Хара Кэя, казалось, утопала в озере тишины. Эрве Жонкур подошел и остановился у входа. Дверей не было вовсе, а на бумажных стенах появлялись и пропадали тени, не поднимавшие ни малейшего шума. Все это едва ли напоминало жизнь. Попытайся он выразить увиденное одним словом, это было бы слово "театр". Эрве Жонкур так и остолбенел у самого дома в ожидании неизвестно чего. За то время, что он предоставил судьбе, лишь тени и безмолвие просачивались за пределы этой необычной сцены. Эрве Жонкур повернулся и ходко пошел к собственному дому. Опустив голову, он смотрел себе под ноги, ибо это помогало ему не думать.

Вечером Эрве Жонкур собрал кладь. Потом дал препроводить себя для обряда омовения в комнату с каменным полом. Он лег, закрыл глаза и подумал о большой вольере — безрассудном залоге любви. На глаза ему положили влажное полотенце. Раньше этого никогда не делали. Он хотел было убрать полотенце, но чья-то рука овладела его рукой и остановила ее. Это не была старая рука старухи.

Эрве Жонкур чувствовал, как по его телу струится вода: сначала по ногам, затем вдоль рук и по груди. Вода словно масло. А вокруг — непривычная тишина. Он ощутил легкое прикосновение шелковой вуали.

[56] И женских рук — женских, нежно обтиравших его кожу повсюду; тех самых рук и того шелка — сотканного из пустоты. Он не шевельнулся, даже когда руки взметнулись с плеч на шею, а пальцы — шелк и пальцы — дотянулись до губ, осторожно притронулись к ним, всего только раз — и растаяли.

Напоследок Эрве Жонкур почувствовал, как шелковая вуаль взлетела над ним и упорхнула без следа. И была рука: она раскрыла его руку и что-то вложила в ладонь.

Он долго ждал в тишине, не шелохнувшись. Затем осторожно снял влажное полотенце с глаз. В комнате почти не было света. Кругом ни души. Он встал, взял сложенную на полу тунику, надел ее, вышел из комнаты и, дойдя до спальни, лег на циновку. Повернув голову, он стал наблюдать за тонким дрожащим пламенем лампы. И бережно остановил Время — на все то время, что хотел.

После этого уже ничего не стоило разжать ладонь и увидеть листок. Маленький. Несколько иероглифов вытянулись в столбик. Черные чернила.

Ранним утром следующего дня Эрве Жонкур пустился в обратный путь. В тайниках своей поклажи он увозил тысячи яичек шелкопряда — будущее Лавильдье, работу для сотен людей и богатство для десятка из них. Там, где дорога сворачивала влево, скрывая за холмистым очерком деревню, он остановился, не обращая внимания на пару провожатых. Спешился и постоял у обочины, глядя на домики, взбиравшиеся по склону холма.

Спустя шесть дней Эрве Жонкур сел в Такаоке на корабль голландских контрабандистов, доставивший его в Сабирк. Оттуда, вдоль китайской границы, он поднялся до

[58] озера Байкал, проделал четыре тысячи верст по сибирским просторам, перевалил через Уральский хребет, добрался до Киева, поездом проехал всю Европу с востока на запад и после трехмесячного путешествия прибыл во Францию. В первое воскресенье апреля — как раз к Праздничной мессе — показался он у въезда в Лавильдье. Навстречу ему выбежала Элен, и он ощутил запах ее кожи, когда обнял жену, и услышал ее бархатный голос, когда она сказала:

— Ты вернулся.

Нежно.

— Ты вернулся.

В Лавильдье текла размеренным чередом нехитрая, обыденная жизнь. Она омывала Эрве Жонкура сорок один день. На сорок второй он не выдержал, достал маленькую укладку из своего дорожного сундука, вынул карту Японии, раскрыл ее и взял упрятанный в ней листок. Несколько иероглифов вытянулись в столбик. Черные чернила. Он сел за письменный стол и долго-долго на них смотрел.

Бальдабью он застал у Вердена, за бильярдом. Бальдабью всегда играл один — против самого себя. Такие вот партии. Здоровяк против калеки, говаривал он сам. Первый удар он делал как обычно, а второй — одной рукой. В тот день, когда победит калека, прибавлял Бальдабью, я навсегда уеду из этих мест. Годами калека проигрывал.

— А что, Бальдабью, нет ли у нас кого, кто маракует по-японски?

Калека закрутил от двух бортов с откатом.

— Спроси у Эрве Жонкура — он все знает.

— Я в этом ни полстолько не смыслю.

— Ты же у нас японец.

— А толку.

Здоровяк согнулся над кием и всадил шестиочковый прямой.

— Тогда остается мадам Бланш. У нее магазин тканей в Ниме. Над магазином бордель. Тоже ее. Она богачка. И японка.

— Японка? А как ее сюда занесло?

— Главное, у самой мадам об этом не спрашивай, если хочешь что-нибудь разузнать. А, че-ерт.

Калека только что смазал четырнадцатиочковый от трех бортов.

Своей Элен Эрве Жонкур сказал, что едет в Ним по делам. И что вернется в тот же день.

Он поднялся во второй этаж магазина тканей по рю Москат, 12, и спросил мадам Бланш. Ждать пришлось долго. Гостиная была обставлена по случаю праздника, начавшегося много лет назад. С тех пор праздник так и не кончался. Все девушки были как на подбор: молоденькие и француженки. Тапер наигрывал под сурдинку мотивчики, отдававшие Россией. В конце каждого из них он запускал в волосы правую руку и приговаривал себе под нос:

— Вуаля.

Эрве Жонкур ждал часа два. Затем его провели по коридору до последней двери. Он открыл ее и вошел.

Мадам Бланш сидела в широком кресле у окна. На ней было легкое кимоно, совершенно белое. Крохотные ярко-голубые цветки увивали ее пальцы, словно кольца. Черные лоснящиеся волосы, безукоризненное восточное лицо.

— Неужели вы и впрямь столь богаты, что вообразили, будто можете лечь со мною в постель?

Эрве Жонкур застыл, сжимая шляпу в руке.

— Я намерен просить вас об одной любезности. Цена не имеет значения.

Он извлек из внутреннего кармана пиджака свернутый вчетверо листок и протянул ей.

— Мне нужно знать, что здесь написано.

Мадам Бланш и бровью не повела. Полусомкнутые губы изготовились к улыбке.

— Прошу вас, мадам.

У нее не было никаких оснований выполнять его просьбу. И все же она взяла листок и, развернув, заглянула в него. Вскинула глаза на Эрве Жонкура и снова их опустила. Медленно сложила листок. Когда она подалась вперед, чтобы вернуть листок, кимоно приоткрылось у нее на груди. Эрве Жонкур успел заметить, что под ним ничего нет и что кожа у нее молодая и белоснежная.

— Вернитесь — или я умру.

Она произнесла это холодным тоном, глядя Эрве Жонкуру прямо в глаза и не выказав ни малейшего чувства.

Вернитесь — или я умру.

Эрве Жонкур убрал листок во внутренний карман пиджака.

— Благодарю.

[64] Коротко поклонившись, он повернулся, подошел к двери и собрался было положить на стол пачку банкнот.

— Пустое.

Эрве Жонкур замялся.

— Я не о деньгах. Я о той женщине. Пустое. Она не умрет. И вы это знаете.

Не оборачиваясь, Эрве Жонкур положил банкноты на стол, отворил дверь и вышел.

Бальдабью говорил, что за ласками мадам Бланш иные приезжали из Парижа. Воротившись в столицу, они вдевали в петлицы фраков крохотные голубые цветки. Те самые, что неизменно увивали ее пальцы, словно кольца.

Тем летом Эрве Жонкур впервые отвез жену на Ривьеру. В Ницце они поселились на две недели в гостинице, облюбованной англичанами и знаменитой своими музыкальными вечерами. Элен внушила себе, что в таком чудесном месте они сумеют зачать ребенка, которого напрасно дожидались много лет. Вместе они решили, что это будет мальчик. И что его нарекут Филиппом. В светской жизни курортного городка они участвовали весьма умеренно, зато потом, уединившись у себя в номере, вовсю потешались над разными чудаками, встреченными за день. Как-то вечером, на концерте, они познакомились с одним поляком, торговцем кожами. Он утверждал, что был в Японии.

Накануне отъезда Эрве Жонкур внезапно проснулся среди ночи. Было еще совсем темно. Он встал и подошел к кровати Элен. Когда она открыла глаза, он услышал, как его голос прошептал:

— Я буду любить тебя вечно.

В начале сентября шелководы Лавильдье устроили сход, чтобы порешить, как быть дальше. Правительство отрядило в Ним молодого биолога для изучения повальной болезни, приводившей в негодность личинки французского шелкопряда. Биолога звали Луи Пастер. Он работал с микроскопами, в которые можно было увидеть невидимое. Поговаривали, будто он уже добился необыкновенных результатов. Из Японии доходили слухи о предстоящей гражданской войне; ее разжигали силы, выступавшие против доступа в Страну иноземцев. В депешах французского консульства, недавно открытого в Иокогаме, рекомендовалось воздержаться от установления торговых отношений с островом — до лучших времен. Склонные к осмотрительности и чувствительные к немалым расходам, в которые выливалась каждая негласная экспедиция в Японию, многие из именитых граждан Лавильдье высказались за то, чтобы приостановить поездки Эрве Жонкура и положиться в этом году на вполне добротные партии шелкопряда от крупных поставщиков с Ближнего Востока. Бальдабью слушал, не проронив ни слова. Под конец настал его черед. Тогда, водрузив свою бамбуковую палку на стол, он обратил взгляд на сидевшего перед ним человека. И стал ждать.

Эрве Жонкур знал о пастеровских изысканиях и читал сообщения, поступавшие из Японии, но говорить об этом всякий раз отказывался. Он почти всецело посвящал себя проекту будущего парка, который собирался разбить вокруг своего дома. В укромном уголке кабинета Эрве Жонкур хранил сложенный вчетверо листок с несколькими иероглифами в столбик — черные чернила. У него был солидный счет в банке, он

[70] вел покойный образ жизни и питал осознанные надежды на то, что вскоре станет отцом. Когда Бальдабью обратил на него взгляд, он лишь сказал:

— Тебе решать, Бальдабью.

Эрве Жонкур отправился в Японию в начале октября. Он пересек границу возле Меца, проехал Вюртемберг и Баварию, въехал в Австрию, поездом добрался до Вены и Будапешта, а затем напрямую до Киева. Отмахал на перекладных две тысячи верст по русской равнине, перевалил через Уральский хребет, углубился в просторы Сибири, сорок дней колесил по ней до озера Байкал, которое в тех краях называют "остатним". Прошел Амур вниз по течению вдоль китайской границы до самого Океана. Дойдя до Океана, просидел в порту Сабирк десять дней, покуда корабль голландских контрабандистов не доставил

4*

его до мыса Тэрая на западном побережье Японии. Возникшая перед ним Страна пребывала в беспокойном ожидании войны, которая никак не могла разразиться. Не один день он провел в пути, отбросив всегдашние предосторожности, ибо география властей и проверок точно рассеялась накануне взрыва, грозившего полностью ее перекроить. В Сиракаве он встретил человека, который должен был отвести его к Хара Кэю. За два дня они доехали верхом до окрестностей деревни. Эрве Жонкур пошел в деревню пешком, чтобы весть о его прибытии докатилась вперед него.

Эрве Жонкура проводили на край деревни, в один из последних домов, на взгорке, прямо у леса. Его дожидались пятеро слуг. Он препоручил им багаж и вышел на веранду. На противоположном конце деревни виднелся дворец Хара Кэя. Немногим больше остальных домов, дворец был окружен гигантскими кедрами, хранившими его уединение. Эрве Жонкур пристально смотрел на этот чертог, словно до самого горизонта ничего больше не было. И вот он увидел, как

внезапно

небо над чертогом окропилось сотнями взлетевших птиц; будто исторгнутая из зем-

[74] ли, невиданная стая разлеталась повсюду, ошеломленная и обезумевшая, щебеча и галдя, — крылатый залп, цветное облако, выпущенное в яркий свет, звонкий фейерверк испуганных звуков, бегущая музыка, полет в небеса.

Эрве Жонкур улыбнулся.

Деревня засуетилась, как ошалевший муравейник. Люди носились и вопили, таращась на небо и провожая взглядом птиц-беглецов. С давних пор птицы являлись гордостью их Господина, и вот теперь они обернулись летящей по небу насмешкой. Эрве Жонкур вышел из дома и не спеша направился через всю деревню, глядя вперед с беспредельным спокойствием. Казалось, никто его не замечает, и он, казалось, не замечает ничего. Под ногами у него бежала золотая нить, пронизавшая уток ковра, вытканного безумцем. Он одолел стянувший реку мост, спустился к исполинским кедрам, вошел в их тень и вышел из тени.

[76] Прямо перед собой он увидал огромную вольеру: створки распахнуты настежь, внутри — пусто. А напротив вольеры — женщину. Не глядя по сторонам, Эрве Жонкур все так же медленно прошел дальше и остановился, лишь когда подступил к ней совсем близко.

У ее глаз не было восточного разреза; ее лицо было лицом девочки.

Эрве Жонкур шагнул ей навстречу, протянул руку и разжал ладонь. На ладони покоился сложенный вчетверо листок. Она скользнула по нему взглядом, и каждый уголок ее лица распустился в улыбку. Затем вложила свою ладонь в ладонь Эрве Жонкура, нежно стиснула ее, чуть-чуть помедлила и убрала руку, сжимая в пальцах обошедший полсвета листок. Не успела она затаить его в складках платья, как раздался голос Хара Кэя.

— Добро пожаловать, мой французский друг.

Хара Кэй стоял в нескольких шагах от них. Темное кимоно, черные волосы идеально собраны на затылке. Он подошел. И перевел взгляд на вольеру, осмотрев одну за другой раскрытые створки.

— Они вернутся. Ведь это так трудно — устоять перед искушением вернуться, не правда ли?

Эрве Жонкур не ответил. Хара Кэй заглянул ему в глаза и вкрадчиво произнес:

— Пойдемте.

Эрве Жонкур последовал за ним. Пройдя немного, он обернулся к девушке и слегка поклонился.

— Надеюсь скоро увидеть вас.

Хара Кэй шел не останавливаясь.

— Она не знает вашего языка.

Сказал он.

— Пойдемте.

34

Вечером Хара Кэй пригласил Эрве Жонкура к себе. В доме уже собрались несколько
поселян. Женщины были одеты с особым
изяществом: густо набеленные лица полы-
хали огненными румянами. Пили саке. Из
длинных деревянных трубок курили едкий
табак с дурманящим запахом. В какой-то
момент появились шуты и человек, забав-
лявший гостей тем, что искусно подражал
голосам людей и животных. Три старухи
играли на струнных инструментах и непре-
станно улыбались. Хара Кэй сидел на почет-
ном месте в темном облачении и с босыми
ногами. Рядом, в сияющем шелковом платье — женщина с лицом девочки. Эрве Жон-

кура усадили в другом конце комнаты. Овеянный приторным ароматом назойливых женщин, он растерянно улыбался мужчинам: те наперебой потчевали его невесть какими баснями, понять которые он был не в состоянии. Стократно он искал ее глаза, и стократно она находила его. То был особый грустный танец, сокровенный и бессильный. Эрве Жонкур кружился в нем до поздней ночи, затем встал, пробормотал по-французски извинения, кое-как отделался от увязавшейся за ним женщины и, пробившись сквозь клубы дыма и скопище тарабаривших говорунов, двинулся к выходу. У порога он в последний раз взглянул на нее. Она не сводила с него безмолвных глаз, отдаленных на столетия.

Эрве Жонкур брел по деревне, вдыхая свежий ночной воздух и плутая в проулках, поднимавшихся по откосу холма. Подойдя к своему дому, он увидел зажженный фонарь, трепетавший за бумажной перегородкой. Он вошел и обнаружил стоявших перед ним двух женщин. Совсем юную девушку восточной наружности, одетую в простое белое кимоно. И ее. В глазах играет лихорадочное веселье. Не дав ему опомниться, она взяла его руку, поднесла ее к своему лицу, легонько коснулась губами, а затем, крепко стиснув, опустила в ладони застывшей рядом девушки и на мгновение придержала, не позволив ей вырваться. Потом она убрала свою руку, отступила на два шага, схватила фонарь, мельком заглянула Эрве Жонкуру в глаза и выбежала. Фонарь был оранжевым. Крохотный бегущий светлячок, он пропал в ночи.

Эрве Жонкур прежде никогда не видел эту девушку; сказать по правде, он не увидел ее и той ночью. В непроглядной комнате он ощутил красоту ее тела, познал ее руки и уста. Он ласкал ее целую вечность, как не ласкал ни разу в жизни, отдавшись на произвол непривычной медлительности. В темноте ничего не стоило любить ее и не любить *ее*.

Незадолго до рассвета девушка встала, набросила белое кимоно и вышла.

Наутро перед домом Эрве Жонкура под-
жидал человек Хара Кэя. При нем было
пятнадцать листов тутовой коры, сплошь
усеянной мельчайшими яичками цвета сло-
новой кости. Эрве Жонкур тщательно ос-
мотрел каждый лист, сговорился в цене и
заплатил сусальным золотом. На прощанье
он дал понять человеку, что хочет повидать-
ся с Хара Кэем. В ответ человек замотал
головой. Жестами он сообщил Эрве Жонкуру, что Хара Кэй покинул деревню на
заре, вместе со свитой, и что никто не знает, когда он вернется.

Эрве Жонкур бросился через всю деревню к жилищу Хара Кэя. Там были одни слу-

ги. На любой вопрос они только качали головами. Дом выглядел опустевшим. И сколько ни всматривался Эрве Жонкур, даже в самых незначительных мелочах он не увидел и намека на оставленное для него послание. По пути в деревню он проходил мимо огромной вольеры. Створки снова были на запоре. Внутри, отгороженные от неба, порхали сотни птиц.

Еще два дня Эрве Жонкур ждал хоть какого-нибудь знака. Затем тронулся в путь.

Примерно в получасе езды от деревни дорога вывела его к лесу, из которого доносился необыкновенный серебристый перезвон. Сквозь густую листву проступали сотни темных пятнышек обосновавшейся на отдых стаи птиц. Ничего не говоря своим проводникам, Эрве Жонкур осадил коня, достал из-за пояса револьвер и дал в воздух шесть выстрелов. Смятенная стая взмыла в небо, подобно облаку дыма, выпущенному пожаром. Облако было таким большим, что виднелось спустя несколько дней пути. Оно чернело в небе уже без всякой на то причины. Если не считать его полнейшей растерянности.

Через шесть дней Эрве Жонкур сел в Такаоке на корабль голландских контрабандистов, доставивший его в Сабирк. Оттуда, вдоль китайской границы, он поднялся до озера Байкал, проделал четыре тысячи верст по сибирским просторам, перевалил через Уральский хребет, добрался до Киева, поездом проехал всю Европу с востока на запад и после трехмесячного путешествия прибыл во Францию. В первое воскресенье апреля — как раз к Праздничной мессе — он показался у въезда в Лавильдье. Остановил экипаж и какое-то время просидел без движения, с опущенными занавесками. Потом вышел и медленно потащился вперед под грузом беспредельной усталости.

Бальдабью спросил у него, видел ли он войну.

— Видел, да не ту, что ждал, — прозвучало в ответ.

Вечером он лег в постель Элен и ласкал ее с таким нетерпением, что она испугалась и не могла сдержать слез. Когда он заметил их, она улыбнулась через силу.

— Просто... я так счастлива, — сказала она тихо.

Эрве Жонкур передал яичную кладку шелководам Лавильдье. После этого он несколько дней кряду не показывался в город-
ке, презрев даже ритуальный променад к
Вердену. В первых числах мая, ко всеобще-
му недоумению, он купил заброшенный
дом Жана Бербека, того самого, что когда-
то умолк и не заговорил уже до самой смерти. Все решили, что Эрве Жонкур надумал
сделать из дома новую лабораторию. А он
и мебель выносить не стал. Только наве-
дывался туда время от времени и подолгу
оставался один в этих комнатах. Неизвестно зачем. Однажды он привел в дом Бальдабью.

— А ты не знаешь, почему Жан Бербек перестал говорить? — спросил у него Эрве Жонкур.

— Об этом и о многом другом он так ничего и не сказал.

Спустя годы на стенах по-прежнему висели картины, а в сушилке у раковины — старые кастрюли. Невеселая картина: будь его воля, Бальдабью охотно бы ретировался. Но Эрве Жонкур как зачарованный пялился на покрытые плесенью мертвые стены. Он явно там что-то выискивал.

— Видно, жизнь иногда поворачивается к тебе таким боком, что и сказать-то больше нечего.

Сказал он.

— Совсем нечего.

Бальдабью не особо тяготел к серьезным разговорам. Он молчаливо разглядывал кровать Жана Бербека.

— В этакой берлоге у кого хочешь язык отнимется.

Долгое время Эрве Жонкур продолжал вести затворнический образ жизни. Он редко показывался на людях и целыми днями работал над проектом парка, который

[90] рано или поздно разобьет вокруг дома. Он покрывал лист за листом странными рисунками, похожими на машины. Как-то под вечер Элен спросила у него:

— Что это?

— Это вольера.

— Вольера?

— Да.

— А для чего она?

Эрве Жонкур не отрывал взгляда от рисунков.

— Ты запустишь в нее птиц, сколько сможешь, а когда в один прекрасный день почувствуешь себя счастливой, откроешь вольеру — и будешь смотреть, как они улетают.

40

В конце июля Эрве Жонкур поехал с женой в Ниццу. Они поселились в маленьком домике на берегу моря. Так захотела Элен. Она не сомневалась, что покой уединенного места развеет хандру, как видно овладевшую мужем. Однако ей хватило проницательности выдать это за свой невольный каприз, подарив любимому сладостную возможность простить ее.

Три недели, проведенные ими вместе, были наполнены простым, неуязвимым счастьем. Когда спадала жара, они нанимали дрожки и забавы ради разъезжали по окрестным деревням, притаившимся на взгорье, откуда море казалось разноцветным

5*

картонным задником. Временами они выбирались в город — на концерт или светский раут. Как-то раз приняли приглашение одного итальянского барона, устроившего по случаю своего шестидесятилетия званый вечер в "Отель Сюис". За десертом Эрве Жонкур нечаянно поднял глаза на Элен. Она сидела напротив, рядом с обольстительным английским джентльменом: в петлице его фрака красовалась гирлянда из крохотных голубых цветков. Эрве Жонкур увидел, как он склонился к Элен и что-то шепчет ей на ухо. Элен залилась упоительным смехом, коснувшись кончиками волос плеча английского джентльмена. В этом движении не было ни капли замешательства, но лишь обескураживающая точность. Эрве Жонкур опустил взгляд на тарелку. Он не мог не подметить, что его рука, зажавшая серебряную десертную ложку, неоспоримо дрожит.

Погодя, в фюмуаре, шатаясь от чрезмерной дозы хмельного, Эрве Жонкур подошел к незнакомому господину. Тот сидел в одиночестве за столом, осоловело вылупив глаза. Эрве Жонкур нагнулся к нему и произнес с расстановкой:

— Должен сообщить вам, сударь, одно весьма важное известие. Мы все отвратительны. Мы все на редкость отвратительны.

Господин был родом из Дрездена. Он торговал телятиной и плохо понимал по-французски. Господин разразился оглушительным смехом и закивал головой. Казалось, он уже никогда не остановится.

Эрве Жонкур и Элен пробыли на Ривьере до начала сентября. Им жаль было покидать маленький домик на берегу моря, ведь в его стенах они почувствовали легкое дыхание любви.

Бальдабью явился к Эрве Жонкуру спозаранку. Они уселись в тени портика.

— Парк-то не сказать чтобы ах.

— Я к нему еще не приступал, Бальдабью.

— Ах.

Бальдабью никогда не курил по утрам. Он вынул трубку, набил ее табаком и раскурил.

— Пообщался я с этим Пастером. Дельный малый. Он мне все показал. Он знает, как отличать больные яички от здоровых. Правда, еще не умеет их лечить. Зато может отбирать здоровые. И говорит, что где-то треть нашего выводка вполне здорова.

Пауза.

— Слыхал — в Японии-то война. На этот раз без осечки. Англичане снабжают оружием правительство, голландцы — восставших. Похоже, они сговорились. Пускай, мол, те хорошенько выложатся, а уж мы потом приберем все к рукам и поделим между собой. Французское консульство знай себе приглядывается. Они только и делают, что приглядываются. Эти умники разве депеши горазды строчить про всякие там смертоубийства да про иностранцев, заколотых как бараны.

Пауза.

— Кофе еще найдется?

Эрве Жонкур налил ему кофе.

Пауза.

— Те двое итальянцев, Феррери и еще один, что прошлым годом подались в Китай... вернулись с отборным товаром, кладка — пятнадцать тысяч унций. В Болле уже взяли партию: говорят, хоть куда. Через месяц снова едут... Предложили нам хорошую сделку, по божеским ценам, одиннадцать франков за унцию, полная страховка. Люди верные, за плечами у них — надежные помощники, пол-Европы товаром оделяют. Верные люди, говорю тебе.

Пауза.

— Не знаю. Авось выдюжим. Вот и своя кладка у нас имеется, и Пастер не зря корпит, и у тех итальянцев, глядишь, чего прикупим... Выдюжим. Народ говорит, что посылать тебя снова — полное неразумие... никаких денег не хватит... а главное, уж очень боязно, и тут они правы, раньше было по-другому, а нынче... нынче оттуда ног не унесешь.

Пауза.

— Короче, они не хотят остаться без кладки, а я — без тебя.

Какое-то время Эрве Жонкур сидел, глядя на несуществующий парк. Затем сделал то, чего не делал никогда.

— Я поеду в Японию, Бальдабью.

Сказал он.

— Я куплю эту кладку. Если понадобится — на свои деньги. А ты решай: вам я ее продам или кому еще.

Такого Бальдабью не ожидал. Все равно как если бы выиграл калека, вогнав последний шар от четырех бортов по неописуемой кривой.

Бальдабью объявил шелководам Лавильдье, что Пастер не заслуживает доверия,
что те двое итальяшек уже облапошили
пол-Европы, что война в Японии кончится
к зиме и что святая Агнесса спросила его
во сне, а не сборище ли они бздунов. Одной Элен он не смог соврать.

— Ему и вправду надо ехать?

— Нет.

— Тогда зачем все это?

— Я не в силах его остановить. Если он
так хочет туда, я могу только дать ему лиш-
ний повод вернуться.

Скрепя сердце шелководы Лавильдье
внесли деньги на экспедицию. Эрве Жон-

[98] кур стал снаряжаться в путь и в первых числах октября был готов к отъезду. Элен, как и в прежние годы, помогала мужу, ни о чем его не спрашивая, утаив свои тревоги. Лишь в последний вечер, задув лампу, она нашла в себе силы сказать:

— Обещай, что вернешься.

Твердым голосом, без всякой нежности.

— Обещай, что вернешься.

В темноте Эрве Жонкур ответил:

— Обещаю.

10 октября 1864 Эрве Жонкур отправился в свое четвертое путешествие в Японию. Он пересек границу возле Меца, проехал Вюртемберг и Баварию, въехал в Австрию, поездом добрался до Вены и Будапешта, а затем напрямую до Киева. Отмахал на перекладных две тысячи верст по русской равнине, перевалил через Уральский хребет, углубился в просторы Сибири, сорок дней колесил по ней до озера Байкал, которое в тех краях называют "святым". Прошел Амур вниз по течению вдоль китайской границы до самого Океана. Дойдя до Океана, просидел в порту Сабирк восемь дней, покуда корабль голландских контра-

бандистов не доставил его до мыса Тэрая на западном побережье Японии. Окольными дорогами проскакал префектуры Исикава, Тояма, Ниигата и вступил в провинцию Фукусима. В Сиракаве он обнаружил полуразрушенный город и гарнизон правительственных войск, окопавшийся в руинах. Он обогнул город с восточной стороны и пять дней напрасно дожидался посланника Хара Кэя. На рассвете шестого дня он выехал в сторону северных холмов. Он продвигался по грубым картам и обрывочным воспоминаниям. После многодневных блужданий он вышел к знакомой реке, а там — к лесу и дороге. Дорога привела его в деревню Хара Кэя. Здесь выгорело все: дома, деревья — все.

Не осталось совсем ничего.

Ни одной живой души.

Эрве Жонкур окаменело смотрел на эту гигантскую погасшую жаровню. Позади у него был путь длиною в восемь тысяч верст. А впереди — пустота.

Он вдруг увидел то, что считал невидимым. Конец света.

44

Эрве Жонкур еще долго оставался в разоренной деревне. Он никак не мог заставить себя уйти, хотя понимал, что каждый час, проведенный там, грозил обернуться катастрофой для него и для всего Лавильдье. Он не добыл яичек шелкопряда, а если и добудет — в запасе у него не больше двух месяцев: за этот срок он должен проехать полсвета, до того как они раскроются в пути, превратившись в массу бесплодных личинок. Опоздай он хоть на день — и крах неизбежен. Все это он прекрасно понимал, но уйти не мог. Так продолжал он сидеть, пока не случилось нечто удивительное и необъяснимое: из пустоты совершенно неожиданно возник мальчик. Одетый в лохмотья, он двигался медленно, с испугом поглядывая на пришельца. Эрве Жонкур не шелохнулся. Мальчик подступил ближе и остановился. Они смотрели друг на друга; их разделяло несколько шагов. Наконец мальчик извлек из-под лохмотьев какой-то предмет, дрожа от страха, подошел к Эрве Жонкуру и протянул ему предмет. Перчатка. Мысленным взором Эрве Жонкур увидел берег озера, сброшенное на землю оранжевое платье и легкие волны: присланные откуда-то издалека, они подгоняли озерную воду к берегу. Он взял перчатку и улыбнулся мальчику.

— Это я — француз... за шелком... француз, понимаешь?.. Это я.

Мальчик перестал дрожать.

— Француз...

В глазах у мальчика блеснули слезы, но он засмеялся. И затарахтел, срываясь на крик. И сорвался с места, жестами призывая Эрве Жонкура следовать за ним. Он скрылся на тропинке, уходившей в лес по направлению к горам.

Эрве Жонкур не сдвинулся с места. Он только вертел в руках перчатку — единственный предмет, доставшийся ему от сгинувшего мира. Он понимал, что уже слишком поздно. И что у него нет выбора.

Он встал. Не спеша подошел к лошади. Вскочил в седло. И проделал то, чего и сам не ожидал. Он сдавил пятками бока животного. И поскакал. К лесу, следом за мальчиком, по ту сторону конца света.

45

Несколько дней они держали путь на север, по горам. Эрве Жонкур не различал дороги: он покорно следовал за своим провожатым и ни о чем его не спрашивал. Так они набрели на две деревни. Завидев пришлых, обитатели прятались в домах, женщины разбегались кто куда. Мальчишка, дико веселясь, выкрикивал им вдогонку какую-то абракадабру на своем наречии. Ему было не больше четырнадцати. Он без устали дул в маленькую бамбуковую свирель, извлекая из нее всевозможные птичьи трели. Вид у него был такой, будто он занят наиглавнейшим делом своей жизни.

На пятый день они достигли вершины холма. Мальчик указал на точку впереди себя: за ней дорога устремлялась вниз. Эрве Жонкур взял бинокль. Увиденное им напоминало некое шествие, состоявшее из вооруженных людей, женщин и детей, повозок и животных. Целая деревня пришла в движение. Эрве Жонкур распознал Хара Кэя на коне, облаченного в темное. За ним покачивался паланкин, занавешенный с четырех сторон пестрой тканью.

Мальчик соскочил с лошади, что-то прорещал напоследок и был таков. Перед тем как скрыться за деревьями, он обернулся и на мгновение замер, пытаясь выразить жестом, что путешествие было прекрасным.

— Путешествие было прекрасным! — крикнул ему Эрве Жонкур.

Весь день Эрве Жонкур следил за караваном издалека. Когда караван расположился на ночлег, он продолжал ехать, не сворачивая с дороги, пока навстречу ему не вышли двое воинов. Они взяли его лошадь и поклажу и отвели Эрве Жонкура в шатер. Он долго ждал. Наконец появился Хара Кэй. Никакого знака приветствия. Он даже не сел.

— Как вы здесь очутились, француз?

Эрве Жонкур не ответил.

— Я спрашиваю, кто вас привел?

Молчание.

— Здесь для вас ничего нет. Только война. И это не ваша война. Уходите.

Эрве Жонкур достал кожаный кошель, открыл его и вытряхнул содержимое на землю. Сусальное золото.

— Война — дорогая игра. Я нужен вам. Вы нужны мне.

Хара Кэй и не взглянул на золотые чешуйки, разметавшиеся по земле. Он повернулся и вышел.

Эрве Жонкур провел ночь на краю лагеря. С ним никто не заговаривал. Никто его словно и не замечал. Люди спали на земле вокруг костров. Всего было два шатра. У одного из них Эрве Жонкур подметил пустой паланкин: с четырех углов свисали небольшие клетки с птицами. К решеткам клеток привязаны маленькие золотые колокольчики. Они легонько позванивали от дуновения ночного ветерка.

Проснувшись, он увидел, что вся деревня собирается выступать. Шатры уже сняли. Открытый паланкин стоял на прежнем месте. Люди молча садились в повозки. Он встал и долго озирался по сторонам: но лишь глаза с восточным разрезом встречались с его глазами и тотчас склоняли взгляд. Он видел вооруженных мужчин и видел детей, которые даже не плакали. Он видел немые лица, какие бывают у гонимых людей. И дерево на обочине. А на суку — повешенного мальчугана. Того, что привел его сюда.

Эрве Жонкур подошел к мальчику и остановился как вкопанный, задержав на нем отрешенный взгляд. Немного погодя он распутал обмотанную вокруг ствола веревку, подхватил тело мальчика, уложил его на землю и опустился перед ним на колени. Он не мог оторвать глаз от этого лица. И не заметил, как деревня тронулась в путь. Он только слышал казавшийся далеким шум каравана, который протянулся совсем рядом — по дороге, уходившей чуть в гору. Он не поднял глаз, даже когда поблизости прозвучал голос Хара Кэя:

— Япония — древняя страна. И законы ее тоже древние. По этим законам двенадцать преступлений караются смертью. Одно из них — доставить любовное послание от своей госпожи.

Эрве Жонкур не отводил взгляда от убитого мальчика.

— У него не было любовных посланий.

— Он *сам* был любовным посланием.

Эрве Жонкур догадался, что к его затылку приставили какой-то предмет, пригнув ему голову к земле.

— Это ружье, француз. Не поднимайте голову, прошу вас.

Эрве Жонкур не сразу понял. Но вот, сквозь смутный гул обращенного в бегство каравана, до слуха его долетел золотистый перезвон тысячи маленьких колокольчиков; звук близился, подступая к нему шаг за шагом, и хоть перед глазами у него была только серая земля, он представил себе, как паланкин качается, подобно маятнику, словно и впрямь видел, как, взбираясь по дороге, он мало-помалу приближался, медленно, но неумолимо, влекомый звуком, который становился все сильнее, невыносимо сильным, и надвигался все ближе, так близко, что можно было его коснуться; позолоченное журчание струилось уже напротив, как раз напротив него — в это мгновение — эта женщина — напротив него.

Эрве Жонкур поднял голову.

Восхитительные ткани, дивные шелка опоясали паланкин. Тысячецветье оранжево-бело-охряно-серебряного. Ни щелочки в волшебном гнезде, только шелестящее колыхание цветов, разлитых в воздухе, — непроницаемых, невесомых, невесомее пустоты.

[112]   Эрве Жонкур не услышал взрыва, разносящего в клочья его жизнь. Он уловил тающий вдали звон, почувствовал, как от затылка отвели ружейный ствол, и разобрал голос Хара Кэя:

— Уходите, француз. И больше не возвращайтесь.

Только тишина на дороге. Тело мальчика на земле. На коленях стоит человек. Покуда брезжит дневной свет.

Эрве Жонкур добирался до Иокогамы одиннадцать дней. Он подмаслил японского чиновника и заполучил шестнадцать кладок яиц шелкопряда, привезенных с юга острова. Эрве Жонкур обернул их шелковой тканью и запломбировал в четырех круглых деревянных коробах. Подыскал суденышко, уходившее на континент, и в первых числах марта высадился на русском берегу. Он двинулся северным путем, чтобы замедлить вызревание яичек и растянуть время, оставшееся до их раскрытия. С вынужденными остановками он проделал четыре тысячи верст по Сибири, перевалил через Урал и прибыл в Санкт-Петер-

бург. Расплатившись золотом, он закупил
сотни пудов льда и погрузил его вместе с
кладкой яиц в трюм торгового судна, взяв-
шего курс на Гамбург. Плавание заняло
шесть дней. Выгрузив четыре круглых деревянных короба, он сел на поезд южного
направления. Через одиннадцать часов
пути, выехав из местечка Геберфельд, поезд остановился для заправки водой. Эрве
Жонкур посмотрел вокруг. По-настоящему
летнее солнце припекало пшеничные поля
и все что ни есть на белом свете. Напротив
Эрве Жонкура сидел русский коммерсант.
Скинув ботинки, он обмахивался последней страницей газеты, набранной по-не-
мецки. Эрве Жонкур взглянул на него по-
внимательнее. Он заметил на его рубашке
мокрые пятна, а на лбу и шее — капли пота.
Русский что-то сказал сквозь смех. Эрве
Жонкур улыбнулся в ответ, встал, ухватил
чемоданы и сошел с поезда. Вернулся в конец состава к товарному вагону, в котором
везли мясо и рыбу, переложенные льдом.
Вода лилась из вагона, как из таза, проды-
рявленного сотней пуль. Он открыл вагон,
залез внутрь, взял один за другим круглые

[116] деревянные короба, вытащил их и разложил на земле у самых рельсов. Закрыл вагон и стал ждать. Когда поезд был готов к отправлению, ему крикнули, чтобы он не мешкал и садился. Он помотал головой и махнул на прощанье рукой. На его глазах поезд уходил все дальше и дальше и вскоре скрылся из виду. Он подождал, пока утихнет всякий шум. Затем наклонился к одному из деревянных коробов, сорвал с него пломбы и вскрыл. То же самое он проделал с тремя другими коробами. Медленно и аккуратно.

Миллионы личинок. Мертвых.

Было 6 мая 1865.

Эрве Жонкур приехал в Лавильдье спустя девять дней. Его жена Элен издали заприметила экипаж, катившийся по аллее поместья. Она сказала себе, что не должна плакать и не должна убегать.

Она спустилась к парадному входу, отпахнула дверь и встала на пороге.

Когда Эрве Жонкур подошел к ней, она улыбнулась. Обняв ее, он тихо сказал:

— Останься со мной, прошу тебя.

Они не смыкали глаз дотемна, сидя на лужайке перед домом, друг возле друга. Элен говорила о Лавильдье, о долгих месяцах ожидания, об ужасе последних дней.

[118]   — Ты умер.
         Сказала она.
         — И на свете не осталось ничего хоро-
шего.

Шелководы Лавильдье взирали на тутовые деревья, покрытые листьями, и видели свою погибель. Бальдабью раздобыл несколько новых кладок, но личинки умирали, едва народившись. Шелка-сырца, полученного от немногих сохранившихся партий, еле хватало, чтобы загрузить две из семи местных прядилен.

— У тебя есть какие-нибудь мысли? — спросил Бальдабью.

— Одна, — ответил Эрве Жонкур.

На следующий день он объявил, что за лето полагает разбить вокруг своего дома парк. И подрядил с десяток-другой односельчан. Те обезлесили пригорок и сгладили уклон, полого спускавшийся теперь в низину. Стараниями работников деревья и живая изгородь исчертили землю легкими, прозрачными лабиринтами. Яркие цветы сплелись в причудливые куртины, открывшиеся словно шутейные прогалины среди березовых рощиц. Вода, позаимствованная из ближней речки, сбегала фонтанным каскадом к западным пределам парка, собираясь в небольшом пруду, обрамленном полянками. В южном урочище, меж лимонных и оливковых деревьев, из дерева и железа соорудили огромную вольеру, казалось, повисшую в воздухе точно вышивка.

Работали четыре месяца. В конце сентября парк был готов. Никто еще в Лавильдье не видывал ничего подобного. Поговаривали, будто Эрве Жонкур пустил на это все свое состояние. Будто вернулся он из Японии каким-то не таким, не иначе как больным. Будто запродал кладку макаронникам и набил мошну золотом, припрятанным в парижских банках. А еще поговаривали, что ежели б не его парк — окочурились бы все с голоду в тот год. И что

был он шельмой. И что был он праведни-
ком. А еще — будто нашло на него что-то,
ровно напасть какая.

О своем странствии Эрве Жонкур сказал только то, что яички шелкопряда раскрылись неподалеку от Кёльна, в местечке под названием Геберфельд.

Спустя четыре месяца и тринадцать дней после его возвращения Бальдабью сел перед ним на берегу пруда у западных пределов парка и сказал:

— Рано или поздно ты все равно расскажешь правду.

Сказал негромко, через силу, ибо сроду не верил, что от правды бывает хоть какая-то польза.

Эрве Жонкур устремил взгляд в сторону парка.

Стояла осень: повсюду разливался обманчивый свет.

— Когда я увидел Хара Кэя в первый раз, на нем была темная туника. Он неподвижно сидел в углу комнаты, скрестив ноги. Рядом лежала женщина. Она положила голову ему на живот. У ее глаз не было восточного разреза. Ее лицо было лицом девочки.

Бальдабью слушал молча. До последнего слова. До поезда из Геберфельда.

Он ни о чем не думал.

Он слушал.

Его кольнуло, когда под конец Эрве Жонкур сказал вполслуха:

— Я даже ни разу не слышал ее голоса.

И, чуть помедлив:

— Какая странная боль.

Тихо.

— Так умирают от тоски по тому, чего не испытают никогда.

Они шли по парку вместе.

Бальдабью произнес всего одну фразу:

— Откуда, черт подери, этот собачий холод?

Всего одну.

Как-то вдруг.

В начале нового, 1866 года Япония официально разрешила вывоз яичек шелковичного червя.

В следующем десятилетии одна лишь Франция будет ввозить японского шелкопряда на десять миллионов франков.

С 1869, после открытия Суэцкого канала, весь путь до Японии займет не больше двадцати дней. И чуть меньше двадцати дней — возвращение.

Искусственный шелк будет запатентован в 1884 французом по фамилии Шардонне.

Спустя полгода после его возвращения в Лавильдье Эрве Жонкуру пришел по почте
конверт горчичного цвета. Вскрыв конверт,
он обнаружил семь листов бумаги, испещ-
ренных мелким геометрическим почерком:
черные чернила, японские иероглифы. Кроме имени и адреса на конверте, в послании
ни слова латинскими буквами. Судя по штем-
пелю, письмо отправили из Остенде.

Эрве Жонкур долго листал и разглядывал его. Письмо напоминало каталог мини-
атюрных птичьих лапок, составленный с
невменяемым усердием. Хотя это были ка-
кие-то значки. Иначе говоря, это был прах
сгоревшего голоса.

Несколько дней подряд Эрве Жонкур носил письмо с собой: сложенное пополам, оно покоилось у него в кармане. Переодеваясь, он всякий раз перекладывал письмо. Но ни разу не заглянул в него. Он лишь ощупывал его рукой, пока говорил с испольщиком или ждал ужина, сидя на веранде. Как-то вечером, у себя в кабинете, он стал рассматривать письмо против лампы. На просвет следы птичек-малюток сливались в глухой, неразборчивый клекот. Они гомонили либо о чем-то пустяковом, либо, напротив, способном перевернуть всю жизнь. Выведать истину было невозможно, и это нравилось Эрве Жонкуру. Появилась

Элен. Он положил письмо на стол. Она подошла поцеловать мужа, как делала каждый вечер, прежде чем удалиться в свою комнату. Когда Элен нагнулась, ночная рубашка слегка разошлась у нее на груди. Эрве Жонкур увидел, что под рубашкой у нее ничего не было и что ее груди были маленькими и белоснежными, как у девочки.

Еще четыре дня он жил привычной жизнью, нисколько не меняя благоразумно заведенного распорядка. Утром пятого дня он надел элегантную серую тройку и поехал в Ним. Сказал, что вернется засветло.

На рю Москат, 12, все было в точности как три года назад. Праздник так и не кончался. Девушки были как на подбор: молоденькие и француженки. Тапер наигрывал под сурдинку мотивчики, отдававшие Россией. То ли от старости, то ли от какой подлой хвори, но он уже не запускал в волосы правую руку и не приговаривал себе под нос:

— Вуаля.

Он только немо замирал, растерянно глядя на свои руки.

Мадам Бланш приняла его без единого слова. Черные лоснящиеся волосы, безукоризненное восточное лицо. На пальцах,
словно кольца, крохотные ярко-голубые
цветки. Длинное белое платье, полупроз-
рачное. Босые ноги.

Эрве Жонкур сел напротив. Вынул из
кармана письмо.

— Вы меня помните?

Мадам Бланш неуловимо кивнула.

— Вы снова мне нужны.

Он протянул ей письмо. У нее не было
ни малейших оснований брать это письмо,
но она взяла его и раскрыла. Проглядев
один за другим все семь листов, она подня-
ла глаза на Эрве Жонкура.

— Я не люблю этот язык, месье. Я хочу его забыть. Я хочу забыть эту землю, и мою жизнь на этой земле, и все остальное.

Эрве Жонкур сидел неподвижно — руки вцепились в ручки кресла.

— Я прочту вам это письмо. Прочту. Денег я с вас не возьму. А возьму только слово: не возвращаться сюда больше и не просить меня об этом.

— Слово, мадам.

Она пристально взглянула на него. Затем опустила взгляд на первую страницу письма: рисовая бумага, черные чернила.

— *Мой любимый, мой господин,*

произнесла она,

— *ничего не бойся, не двигайся и молчи, нас никто не увидит.*

Оставайся так, я хочу смотрѣть на тебя, я
столько на тебя смотрела, но ты был не моим,
сейчас ты мой, не подходи, прошу тебя, побудь
как есть, впереди у нас целая ночь, и я хочу смот-
рѣть на тебя, я еще не видела тебя таким, твое
тело — мое, твоя кожа, закрой глаза и ласкай
себя, прошу,

— мадам Бланш говорила, Эрве Жонкур слушал —

не открывай глаза, если можешь, и ласкай себя,
у тебя такие красивые руки, они столько раз сни-
лись мне, теперь я хочу видеть их, мне приятно
видеть их на твоей коже, вот так, прошу тебя,

[132] *продолжай, не открывай глаза, я здесь, нас никто не видит, я рядом, ласкай себя, мой любимый, мой господин, ласкай себя внизу живота, прошу тебя, не спеши,*

— она остановилась; пожалуйста, дальше, сказал он —

она так хороша – твоя рука на твоем члене, не останавливайся, мне нравится смотреть на нее и смотреть на тебя, мой любимый, мой господин, не открывай глаза, не сейчас, тебе не надо бояться, я рядом, ты слышишь? я здесь, я могу коснуться тебя, это шелк, ты чувствуешь? это мое шелковое платье, не открывай глаза, и ты познаешь мою кожу,

— она читала не торопясь, голосом женщины-девочки —

ты изведаешь мои губы; в первый раз я коснусь тебя губами, и ты не поймешь, где именно, ты вдруг почувствуешь тепло моих губ и не сможешь понять где, если не откроешь глаза, – не открывай их, и ты почувствуешь мои губы совсем внезапно,

— он слушал неподвижно; из кармашка серой тройки выглядывал белоснежный платок —

быть может, на твоих глазах: я прильну губами к твоим векам и бровям, и ты почувствуешь, как мое тепло проникает в твою голову, а мои губы – в твои глаза; а может, ты почувствуешь их на твоем члене: я приложусь к нему губами и постепенно их разомкну, спускаясь все ниже и ниже,

— она говорила, склонившись над листами и осторожно касаясь рукой шеи —

и твой член раскроет мои уста, проникая меж губ и тесня язык, моя слюна стечет по твоей коже и увлажнит твою руку, мой поцелуй и твоя рука сомкнутся на твоем члене одно в одном,

— он слушал, не сводя глаз с пустой серебряной рамы, висевшей на стене —

а под конец я поцелую тебя в сердце, потому что хочу тебя; я вопьюсь в кожу, что бьется на твоем сердце, потому что хочу тебя, и твое сердце

[134] *будет на моих устах, и ты будешь моим, весь, без остатка, и мои уста сомкнутся на твоем сердце, и ты будешь моим, навсегда; если не веришь – открой глаза, мой любимый, мой господин, и посмотри на меня: это я, разве кому-то под силу перечеркнуть теперешний миг и мое тело, уже не обвитое шелком, и твои руки на моем теле, и устремленный на меня взгляд,*

— она говорила, подавшись к лампе; пламенный свет заливал бумагу, сочась сквозь ставшее прозрачным платье —

твои пальцы у меня внутри, твой язык на моих губах, ты скользишь подо мной, берешь меня за бедра, приподнимаешь и плавно сажаешь меня на свой член; кто сможет перечеркнуть все это: ты медленно движешься внутри меня, твои ладони на моем лице, твои пальцы у меня во рту, наслаждение в твоих глазах, твой голос, ты движешься медленно, но все же делаешь мне больно – и так приятно, мой голос,

— он слушал; в какое-то мгновение он обернулся к ней, увидел ее, попробовал опустить глаза, и не смог —

мое тело на твоем, выгибаясь, ты легонько подбрасываешь его, твои руки удерживают меня, я чувствую внутри себя удары — это сладостное исступление, я вижу, как твои глаза пытливо всматриваются в мои, чтобы понять, докуда мне можно сделать больно: докуда хочешь, мой любимый, мой господин, этому нет предела и не будет, ты видишь? никто не сможет перечеркнуть теперешний миг, и ты вечно будешь с криком закидывать голову, я вечно буду закрывать глаза, смахивая слезы с ресниц, мой голос в твоем голосе, ты удерживаешь меня в своем неистовстве, и мне уже не вырваться, не отступиться, ни времени, ни сил больше нет, этот миг должен был настать, и вот он настал, верь мне, мой любимый, мой господин, этот миг пребудет отныне и вовек, и так до скончания времен.

— она говорила чуть слышно и наконец умолкла.

На листе, который она держала в руке, не было других знаков: тот был последним. Однако, повернув лист, чтобы положить его, она увидела на обратной стороне еще несколько аккуратно выведенных строк — черные чернила посреди белого поля страницы. Она вскинула глаза на Эрве Жонкура. Он смотрел на нее проникновенным взглядом, и она поняла, какие прекрасные у него глаза. Она опустила взгляд на лист.

– *Мы больше не увидимся, мой господин.*

— сказала она —

Положенное нам мы сотворили, и вы это знаете. Верьте: сделанное нами останется навсегда. Живите своей жизнью вдали от меня. Когда же так будет нужно для вашего счастья, не раздумывая забудьте об этой женщине, которая без сожаления говорит вам сейчас "прощай".

Некоторое время она еще смотрела на лист бумаги, затем присоединила его к остальным, возле себя, на столике светлого дерева. Эрве Жонкур сидел не двигаясь. Он лишь повернул голову и опустил глаза, невозмутимо уставившись на едва намеченную, но безукоризненную складку, пробороздившую его правую брючину от паха до колена.

Мадам Бланш встала, нагнулась к лампе и потушила ее. В комнате теплился слабый свет, проникавший туда через круглое окошко. Она приблизилась к Эрве Жонкуру, сняла с пальца кольцо из крохотных голубых цветков и положила его рядом с ним. Потом сделала несколько шагов, отворила маленькую расписную дверцу, спрятанную в стене, и удалилась, оставив дверцу полуоткрытой.

Эрве Жонкур долго сидел в этом необыкновенном свете и все вертел в руках цветочное кольцо. Из гостиной доносились звуки усталого рояля: они растворяли время почти до неузнаваемости.

Наконец он встал, подошел к столику светлого дерева, собрал семь листов рисовой бумаги. Пересек комнату, не глядя миновал полуоткрытую дверцу и вышел.

В последующие годы Эрве Жонкур избрал для себя тот ясный образ жизни, какой пристал человеку, не ведавшему нужды. Он коротал дни под опекой размеренных переживаний. В Лавильдье, как и прежде, восхищались этим человеком, ибо видели в нем воплощение *правильной* жизни, к которой и следует стремиться на этом свете. Говаривали, что таким он был и в молодости, до хождений в Японию.

Он взял за правило совершать раз в год небольшое путешествие со своей женой Элен. Они повидали Неаполь, Рим, Мадрид, Мюнхен, Лондон. Однажды добрались до самой Праги, где все казалось им театром. Они путешествовали, не считаясь со временем и не строя заранее планов. Их поражало все: втайне, даже собственное счастье. Когда они начинали тосковать по тишине, то возвращались в Лавильдье.

Спроси его кто-нибудь, Эрве Жонкур ответил бы, что они готовы жить так вечно. Он источал совершенное умиротворение, как человек, живущий в согласии с собой. Иногда, ветреным днем, он выходил в парк, спускался к пруду и часами просиживал на берегу, глядя, как рябь на воде слагается в необычайные фигуры, играющие то тут, то там шальным блеском. Повсюду веял все тот же ветер, но при взгляде на водную гладь казалось, что их тысяча. От края до края. Пленительная картина. Легкая и необъяснимая.

Иногда, ветреным днем, Эрве Жонкур спускался к пруду и часами смотрел на воду, расчерченную легкими и необъяснимыми картинами, в которые слагалась его жизнь.

16 июня 1871, ближе к полудню, в дальней части кабачка Вердена, калека закатил дурака от четырех бортов с откатом. Потрясенный Бальдабью оцепенел, согнувшись над столом: одна рука отъехала за спину, другая все еще сжимала кий.

— Вот те на.

Он распрямился, положил кий и, не сказав ни слова, вышел. Через три дня Бальдабью уехал. Обе свои прядильни он подарил Эрве Жонкуру.

— О шелке я больше знать ничего не желаю, Бальдабью.

— Продай их, дурень.

Никому так и не удалось у него выудить,

куда это он вдруг наладился. И на кой черт. Он что-то там промямлил насчет святой Агнессы, но никто толком не понял.

В день отъезда Эрве Жонкур и Элен проводили его на вокзал в Авиньоне. При нем имелся всего один чемодан, что, в общем, тоже было маловразумительно. Увидав пыхтевший у перрона поезд, он опустил чемодан на землю.

— Знавал я одного оригинала, который проложил железную дорогу для себя одного.

Сказал он.

— Самое интересное, что она была совершенно прямой: сотни верст без единого поворота. На то была какая-то причина, только уже не помню какая. Вечно эти причины забываются. Ну да ладно, прощайте.

Он не особо тяготел к серьезным разговорам. А прощание, как ни крути, разговор серьезный.

Они смотрели, как он удаляется: он и его чемодан. Навсегда.

И тут Элен совершила нечто странное. Отпрянув от Эрве Жонкура, она кинулась вслед за Бальдабью. Догнала его, крепко обняла и разрыдалась.

[142]   Элен вообще-то никогда не плакала.

Эрве Жонкур продал обе прядильни за бесценок Мишелю Ларио. Душа человек. Двадцать лет, каждую субботу, он с несокрушимым постоянством продувал Бальдабью в домино. У него было три дочери. Первых двух звали Флоранс и Сильвия. Зато третью — Агнесса.

Три года спустя, зимой 1874, Элен заболела воспалением мозга. Врачи не смогли ни объяснить, ни вылечить его. Она умерла в начале марта. Дождливым днем.

Проститься с ней пришли все жители Лавильдье. Они молча поднимались по кладбищенской аллее. Элен была светлым человеком и не принесла никому горя.

Эрве Жонкур велел выбить на ее могиле одно-единственное слово:

Hélas[1].

Он всех благодарил, то и дело твердя, что ему ничего не нужно, и вернулся домой.

---

1 Увы (*франц.*).

[144] Никогда еще дом не казался Эрве Жонку-ру таким большим. А его судьба — такой бес-связной.

Поскольку отчаяние было крайностью ему не свойственной, он сосредоточился на том, что осталось от его жизни, и снова начал ухаживать за ней с неумолимым упор-ством садовника, берущегося за работу на-утро после бури.

Однажды, спустя два месяца и одиннадцать дней после смерти Элен, Эрве Жонкур пошел на кладбище. Рядом с розами, которые он приносил на могилу жены каждую неделю, Эрве Жонкур увидел венчик из крохотных голубых цветков. Нагнувшись, он стал рассматривать их и долго еще пребывал в таком положении. Случись кому застигнуть эту сцену, она наверняка показалась бы ему странноватой, если не сказать смешной. Придя домой, Эрве Жонкур, против обыкновения, уже не выходил работать в парк, а сел в кабинете и задумался. С утра до вечера он только то и делал. Думал.

64

На рю Москат, 12, он обнаружил ателье. Ему сказали, что мадам Бланш давно здесь не живет. Он узнал, что она переехала в Париж и стала содержанкой какого-то высокопоставленного лица, вероятно политика.

Эрве Жонкур выехал в Париж.

На поиски адреса ушло шесть дней. Он послал ей записку с просьбой о встрече. Она ответила, что ждет его в четыре пополудни следующего дня. Точно в назначенный час он поднялся в третий этаж изящного особняка на бульваре Капуцинок. Дверь открыла горничная. Она провела его в гостиную. Мадам Бланш появилась в очень элегантном и очень французском платье. Волосы ниспадали ей на плечи, сообразно тогдашней парижской моде. Колец из голубых цветков на руках не было. Она села против Эрве Жонкура, не говоря ни слова. И замерла в ожидании.

Он посмотрел ей в глаза, как посмотрел бы ребенок.

— Ведь это вы написали то письмо, не правда ли?

Сказал он.

— Элен попросила вас написать, и вы написали.

Мадам Бланш сидела, затаив дыхание, не отводя глаз, не выдавая ни малейшего волнения.

Наконец она промолвила:

— Письмо писала не я.

Молчание.

— Его написала Элен.

Молчание.

— Когда она пришла ко мне, оно уже было написано. Она попросила меня переложить письмо на японский. И я согласилась. Вот как все было.

В этот момент Эрве Жонкур понял, что будет слышать ее слова всю свою жизнь. Он встал и продолжал стоять, словно вдруг позабыл, куда идти. Откуда-то издалека донесся голос мадам Бланш:

— А еще она захотела прочесть его. У нее был чарующий голос. Она произносила эти слова с таким волнением, которого мне не забыть никогда. Как будто это были ее настоящие слова.

Эрве Жонкур шел по гостиной, еле волоча ноги.

— Видите ли, месье, я думаю, что больше всего на свете ей хотелось *стать той женщиной*. Вам этого не понять. А я слышала, как она читает свое письмо. И знаю, что это так.

Эрве Жонкур подошел к двери, взялся за ручку и, не оборачиваясь, выдохнул:

— Прощайте, мадам.

Это была их последняя встреча.

Эрве Жонкур прожил еще двадцать три года. Бо́льшую часть из них — в добром здравии и душевном покое. Он уже никуда не уезжал из Лавильдье и не покидал своего дома. Он мудро распоряжался своим состоянием, и это избавило его от необходимости работать где бы то ни было, кроме собственного парка. Со временем он стал позволять себе удовольствие, в котором раньше всегда отказывал: навещавшим его он описывал свои путешествия. Слушая эти рассказы, жители Лавильдье познавали мир, а дети постигали чудо. Говорил он медленно, замечая в воздухе то, чего другие не замечали.

[150]   По воскресеньям он выбирался в город к Праздничной мессе. Раз в году объезжал местные прядильни, чтобы потрогать новорожденный шелк. Когда одиночество сжимало ему сердце, он приходил на кладбище поговорить с Элен. Остаток времени он проводил в кругу обрядовых привычек, ограждавших его от уныния. Иногда, ветреным днем, он спускался к пруду и часами смотрел на воду, расчерченную легкими и необъяснимыми картинами, в которые слагалась его жизнь.

Алессандро Барикко
Шёлк

Директор издательства С.Пархоменко

Главный редактор В.Горностаева

Художник А.Бондаренко

Ответственный за выпуск В.Бару

Технический редактор Л.Синицына

Корректор Г.Пятышева

Изд. лиц. ИД № 02194 от 30.06.2000 "Иностранка".
Подписано в печать 01.02.2005. Формат $70×100^1/_{32}$.
Бумага газетная пухлая. Гарнитура "New Baskerville".
Печать офсетная. Усл. печ. л. 6,13.
Уч.-изд. л. 4,28. Тираж 5000 экз. Заказ № 65.

Издательство "Иностранка"
119017, Москва, ул. Пятницкая, 41
www. inostranka.ru
e-mail: mail@inostranka.ru

Отпечатано с готовых диапозитивов
на ФГУИПП "Уральский рабочий"
620219, Екатеринбург, ул. Тургенева, 13
www.uralprint.ru
e-mail: book@uralprint.ru

По вопросам оптового приобретения книг
издательства "ИНОСТРАНКА" обращаться:

ООО ИЗДАТЕЛЬСТВО "ИНОСТРАНКА"
    тел.: (095) 953-3580
    факс: (095) 959-5543
    sale@inostranka.ru
    www.inostranka.ru

ООО "ИЗДАТЕЛЬСТВО "У-ФАКТОРИЯ"
    тел.: (343) 257-4292; 257-8589
    факс: (343) 257-8535
    kniga@ufactory.ru
    www.ufactory.ru

ООО "ФИРМА "СТОЛИЦА СЕРВИС"
    тел: (095) 375-3673; 375-2433; 375-3211
    stolitsa@front.ru
    www.stolitsa-books.narod.ru

Editor	Consulting Editor
Gary Carey, M.A.	*James L. Roberts, Ph.D.*
University of Colorado	*Department of English*
	University of Nebraska

ISBN 0-8220-1224-3
© Copyright 1988
by
Cliffs Notes, Inc.
All Rights Reserved
Printed in U.S.A.

1999 Printing

The Cliffs Notes logo, the names "Cliffs" and "Cliffs Notes," and the black and yellow diagonal-stripe cover design are all registered trademarks belonging to Cliffs Notes, Inc., and may not be used in whole or in part without written permission.

Cliffs Notes, Inc.   Lincoln, Nebraska

STEPPENWOLF & SIDDHARTHA

NOTES

including
- *Life and Background*
- *Introductions to* Steppenwolf *and* Siddhartha
- *Lists of Characters*
- *Critical Commentaries*
- *Character Analyses*
- *Review Questions*
- *Selected Bibliography*

by
Carolyn Roberts Welch, M.A.
Associate Professor of English
Quinsigamond Community College

FINKELSTEIN
MEMORIAL LIBRARY
SPRING VALLEY, N.Y.

INCORPORATED

LINCOLN, NEBRASKA 68501

3 2191 00583 4329

CONTENTS

Character Analyses

Review Questions

Selected Bibliography

Life and Background

Even though Hermann Hesse belongs to German literature because of his language and culture, his background is quite unlike that of most German authors. This is due in part to the fact that Hesse had missionary parents and grandparents, and is due in part, also, to the fact that his mother and father were, respectively, of southern German plus French-Swiss stock and northern German plus Slavic stock. Born in the Black Forest town of Calw in the German grand duchy of Württemberg in 1877, Hesse was, paradoxically, reared in the severe austerity of Pietist German Protestantism and yet, at the same time, was suffused in the languages, lore, and mysticism of the Far East. The interaction of these elements influenced Hesse's entire life.

To understand *Siddhartha* and *Steppenwolf,* one should continually be aware of the process of synthesis, a mental process of reconciling dualities of antithetical elements. Hesse became aware of this process of unifying opposites during his period of psychoanalysis under Dr. Joseph Bernhard Lang and Lang's mentor, Dr. Carl Gustav Jung. We can see this process at work in his psychoanalytic and post-psychoanalytic literature (including *Siddhartha* and *Steppenwolf*), in which the theme of self-quest by resolving chaotic polar opposites appears.

Hermann Hesse's long lifetime (1877-1962) spanned the rise of the post-Bismarkian military-industrial complex, the rise of fanatical right-wing extremism, two traumatic world wars, the plague of Nazism which sent his wife's family to extermination, and the Cold War. Hesse deplored industrialism, right-wing nationalism, and war, and, for these reasons, he left Germany to live in the seclusion of Switzerland from 1912 to his death in 1962.

Hesse's works are difficult, different, and unlike most of the works of Western writers. But Hesse was different, even from

the beginning. His father, Johannes Hesse, was a Pietist missionary who renounced his Russian citizenship to become a
Swiss citizen and pursue the theological studies at the Basel
Mission Society. Like his father, Hermann Hesse was also to
renounce his own citizenship — in his case German, which he
held from 1891 to 1923 — when he resumed his Swiss citizenship
and became naturalized. Both of Hesse's parents had very close
contact, through their missionary work, with India and the Far
East. His mother was, in fact, born in India, and his grandmother
was remembered for her striking collection of Eastern garb, arti-
facts, and religious objects. Hermann's grandfather was a highly
renowned missionary and a veritable walking encyclopedia of
Eastern lore and languages. He served as a missionary to the
East for thirty years and his home exuded the flavors of Indian,
Buddhist, and Mohammedian ceremonies, Oriental songs, and
unusual stories and folklore.

Among the significant impressions and experiences of
Hesse's early years were those associated with formal education
and educational institutions, particularly those in 1892 at the
Protestant Theological Seminary at Maulbronn. Hesse's life in
school was turbulent. He hated school and was truant and de-
linquent upon more than one occasion. During his school days
he became conscious of two antithetical worlds — one, the world
of mediocrity upheld by the authoritarian establishment of the
school system; the other, the world of greatness and genius that
this very same establishment supposedly represented. Already
we can see the dichotomy of the mundane bourgeois world and
the world of the Immortals. It is in *Under the Wheel* (1906) that
Hesse depicts his vivid memories of unhappy school days in a
story concerning a student's processes of mental exhaustion and
suicide for which the school system is held blameworthy. After
a period of school truancy and delinquency at Maulbronn and at
Constance, Hesse worked in a bookstore as an apprentice in
Esslingen for only three days and then assisted his father in the
Calw publishing house until 1895. He began his career in poetry
during the four-year period in Tübingen from 1895 to 1899, during which he held a conventional apprenticeship in the Hecken-
hauer Bookshop. *Romantic Songs* was published in 1899

Between 1899 and 1903, Hesse spent time in Calw and Gaien-hofen, but spent his busiest years of this period in Basel. These years are marked by *An Hour Beyond Midnight* (1899) and *Hermann Lauscher* (1901) which, like the bulk of Hesse's early works, bear out the German Romantic tradition of lingering melancholy, gentle fantasy, and lyrical beauty. In 1902, Hesse's mother died, and in 1903, he had quit the book business entirely and was devoting his full energies to writing.

The 1904-12 period was a prolific one, during which his writing style hardened into realism. This period was largely spent in Gaienhofen, and it was during this time that Hesse had his first literary success in the novel *Peter Camenzind* (1904), for which he received his first award. It was in 1904, also, that Hesse married Maria Bernouelli and settled with her on Lake Constance. The year 1905 heralded Hesse's founding of the liberal weekly periodical *März*, which he edited and to which he contributed liberal material until 1912. Other works of the 1904-12 period include *Under the Wheel* (1906); volumes of short stories, including *In This World* and *Neighbors* (1907, 1909); the novel *Gertrude* (1910); and a volume of poetry in 1911. During 1911 and 1912, Hesse's long interest in the East resulted in his traveling to India in search of peace and timelessness beyond the world of Western man. He conveyed this mystical vision in two later works, *Siddhartha* (1922) and *The Journey to the East* (1931); interestingly, his memoirs of the trip, *From India* (1913), contain a sense of disillusionment, a feeling that India was already too Westernized. Some critics feel that Hesse had begun to doubt the validity of missionary work, believing that it was Western man's attempt to do away with Eastern gods.

The period between 1912 and 1919 was a grim period in Hesse's life for it included a succession of psychoanalytic sessions. This was the period during which he made Switzerland his permanent home, living in Bern from 1912 until 1919, when he moved to Montagnola, where he lived for the rest of his life. The primary causes of this period's grimness were his father's death (1916), the long illness of his youngest son, his wife's insanity (note Haller's wife in *Steppenwolf*), and the outbreak of World

War I (1914). Hesse was exempted from active combat duty due
to his poor eyesight, but he was assigned to the German em-
bassy at Bern to work on behalf of German prisoners of war. It
was during these war years that Hesse's pacifism became em-
phatically articulate and politically committed. As a result of his
anti-war articles, some of which are profoundly beautiful, the
right-wing press excoriated Hesse and labeled him a traitor. The
fever of nationalism was so rampant that many of his subscribers
refused to buy or sell his work. The materials of this period include a variety of short stories, poems, and a significant series of
articles for German prisoners of war in the newspaper *Deutsche
Internierten Zeitung*. The horror with which Hesse viewed World
War I cannot be underestimated and the amount of his anti-war
material is quite large. Anti-war activities included his co-editor-
ship of the pacifist periodical *Vivos Voco* and his directorship of
the bi-weekly *Sunday Courier for German Prisoners of War*.
Notable are his "Friends, Do Not Speak in These Tones!" (1914),
the title of which alludes to one of Schiller's poems. It was the
impact of these events between 1912 and 1919, especially the
war, which drew Hesse to consultations with Dr. Lang and Dr.
Jung, two men who were to have a profound synthesizing effect
on his mind and art. The works which came as a result of this
period of psychoanalysis were considerably more introspective
than any of Hesse's previous publications. Works of this period
include *Rosshalde* (1914), *Demian* (1919), the beginnings of
Siddhartha, and a collection of three essays, *In Sight of Chaos*
(1919). Hesse, indeed, had his own glimpse into chaos while
undergoing psychoanalysis, and the essays in *In Sight of Chaos*
dealt with the theme of antithetical God/Satanism in man and
the idea that irrational depravity lurks beneath the surface of
man, collectively as well as individually. Hesse forecast that
these irrational forces would rise to the surface and beget the
criminality which would beset not only Germany, but mankind
as a whole. The outstanding essays in this collection influenced
T. S. Eliot's *Waste Land* (1922), and several references to Hesse
appear in Eliot's notes. The most brilliant essay of the three is
"The Brothers Karamazov, or the Downfall of Europe."

The years from 1919 to 1962 encompass the time from which
Hesse became a naturalized Swiss citizen (1923, also the year of

his divorce from his first wife) to the time of his death on August 9, 1962. From 1919 on, he lived in the same secluded villa on the edge of Montagnola in the Ticino valley into which he invited very few visitors. During this time, Hesse embarked on, as it were, a period of self-quest, using certain theories of Jung. The idea of self-quest (through synthesis) begins in *Demian* and continues through a number of Bildungsroman-type, semi-autobiographical novels; this is the period of *Klein and Wagner* (1920); *Klingsor's Last Summer* (1920); the literary experiment dealing with self-exorcism, *Steppenwolf* (1927); *Crisis* (1928), the verse counterpart to *Steppenwolf; Narcissus and Goldmund* (1930); and *The Journey to the East* (1931). In 1924, Hesse married Ruth Wenger, and after his divorce from her, he married Ninon Ausländer with whom he lived until his death.

After 1931, Hesse's literary output diminished. It was, however, during this time that he wrote a major volume of poetry, published in 1942, completed a new edition of *Steppenwolf,* containing his own introduction, and spent a decade preparing the masterpiece which accounted largely for his winning the Nobel Prize for Literature in 1946, *The Glass Bead Game* (1943). This period also included *War and Peace* (1946), a volume of essays; and *Letters* (1951), a collection of correspondences. During World War II, while Hesse was writing for Will Vesper's *Neue Litteratur,* he was again reviled by Germany's right-wing press. Hesse, however, was not dealt with as severely as was Thomas Mann, whose books were officially burned and who escaped to the United States; Hesse was discounted as merely a "victim of Jewish psychoanalysis" and was not granted paper or other materials for publishing. Hesse's wife's family was not so lucky; they were murdered in the extermination camps by the Nazis. The bitterness and shock that resulted remained with Hesse for the rest of his life.

Steppenwolf Notes

INTRODUCTION

Steppenwolf, published in 1927, is an offbeat but decorous little novel. At times, it is structurally reminiscent of Goethe's *Sorrows of Young Werther* in its use of the notebook device; in places, it is philosophically reminiscent of *Siddhartha,* although it is more ambivalent in conception and, unlike *Siddhartha,* it has an unresolved ending. What Hesse created in *Steppenwolf* was a novel in which the text departed increasingly from reality into fantasy, without intrusions in the narrative announcing the protagonist's traversing the boundary between these disparate worlds. Reality and fantasy are unobtrusively fused into one another by an accumulation of motifs which are forcefully recapitulated in the Magic Theater sequence.

Harry Haller's notes are presented as recorded internal monologue, spontaneous inner autobiography showing the chaotic and schizophrenic qualities of Haller's fantasies. The wolf of the steppes, *der Steppenwolf,* represents the dark, suppressed, rebellious side of Haller's personality. It lies dormant at times, but frequently stalks and threatens Haller's inclination toward bourgeois life and tastes. Haller's records present both Haller's inclination toward the ordered world and the Steppenwolf's inclination toward rebelliousness, art, and flights into imagination. His vision of art, which reaches its highest form in music, is that of art as an end in itself—the Kantian ideal of art for art's sake, which runs exactly counter to the Bürger's ideals of practicality and technical progress. This is not all that Haller's records reveal, however. They progress and finally end problematically—that is, the resolution concerns not just a split personality, but a multiple personality. To Hesse, this was the human condition of not just Harry Haller, but of twentieth-century man. The notes of Haller depart increasingly from reality as they progress, reflecting a syndrome of dissolution as Hesse and Haller partake of their own glimpses into personal and collective chaos. We should not, however, regard *Steppenwolf* as just a *roman à clef,* an exact parallel to the author's life. Rather, we should regard it as a creative work in its own right despite its heavy overlay of autobiography.

The bulk of the accumulating images in *Steppenwolf* are basically Jungian, as are the processes of self-realization and the approach toward equilibrium. Yet *Steppenwolf,* it should be pointed out, presents only an *approach* toward equilibrium. The ending of the novel, despite its promise of impending stabilization for Haller, is unlike the ending of *Siddhartha* in that it is unresolved and technically dissonant.

The technique of *Steppenwolf* places heavy demands upon a translator because the work is a kind of experiment in atonality, in unresolved dissonance. The work has been said to be symphonic in form, which indeed it is; but the mark of such innovative composers as Arnold Schönberg (Austrian, 1874-1951) and Alban Berg (Austrian, 1885-1935) has been unmistakably left on *Steppenwolf.* Schönberg abandoned tonality completely in his "Three Piano Pieces" (Op. 11) of 1908, and had devised the atonal twelve-tone scale by 1915. Shortly thereafter, Alban Berg composed a startlingly dissonant opera, *Wozzeck* (produced in Berlin in 1925), which contains striking combinations of symphonic form and radical atonality.

As far as the novel is concerned, we should note that its technique of verbal and syntactical dissonance rises when departures into unreality are made. The book begins in an unobtrusive realistic style, in keeping with events in the early parts of the book. As the novel progresses, however, and as the departures from reality become more frequent and striking, the prose technique changes accordingly. It becomes more symbolic and the first-person narrative of Haller eventually approximates a stream-of-consciousness technique in the Magic Theater sequence. The first hints at a departure from reality come when Haller discovers a previously unnoticed, visionary gate in a churchyard wall; he imagines that he sees fleeting iridescent letters above the gate, advertising entertainments for madmen.

Further departure from reality becomes apparent in Haller's dream of Goethe, laughing. The final sequence of unreality concerns Hermine's and Pablo's attempts to cure Haller by means of mirrors (the "trifling suicide," the extinguishing of the will in Schopenhaurean terms; the ego in Jungian terms) and the subsequent fragmentation and potential synthesis of Haller's thousandfold personality in the psychoanalytic shock therapy of the Magic Theater sequence. Of primary significance, of course, is the "golden thread" or "golden trace" which draws Haller to Mozart. As we explore the novel, we should be particularly conscious of the interplay of elements derived from Arthur Schopenhauer's *The World as Will and Idea* (1818), including his concepts of will, intellect, individuation and Nirvana. If we couple Schopenhauer's thought with Jung's, bearing in mind the influence upon each of Eastern mysticism, we may then find a critical basis on which to build an understanding of what possibly makes Haller "tick." The polarity of will and intellect plus the Nietzschean theory of man's being driven by a will to power and perfection is basic to much of the art and literature of Germany's twentieth century.

LIST OF CHARACTERS

Harry Haller

The disillusioned protagonist who, according to the nephew, has left behind a collection of notes embodying the *Weltschmerz* of the twentieth-century artist-type.

The Nephew

To some people, he may seem to be the perpetrator of a publishing hoax, but, to others, he is a young businessman whose affinity to the phantom-like Haller draws him to salvage and interpret the bizarre, abandoned manuscript.

The Aunt

A kindly, maternal embodiment of the positive values of the pre-decadent, nineteenth-century middle class. She accepts Haller and elicits interesting philosophical responses from him which are recorded in the manuscript.

The Peddler

An eerie encounter between Haller and the peddler, which is recorded in the manuscript, anticipates the first departure from reality and portends the Magic Theater sequence.

Hermine

Psychologically, this character from the commercial, worldly realm functions as Haller's "double," the reverse of his disciplined and contemplative self. As his Jungian "anima," or female self, she serves as his mentor in the realm of illusion and gives him the perspective to apprehend a reality transcending the illusory.

Maria

An attractive young girl who is Hermine's disciple in the realm of illusion; she attempts to teach love as a kind of art.

Pablo

The guru of the world of commercial jazz and of voyages into artificially induced fantasy; he is the leader of a corrupt realm but extends to Haller a firsthand awareness of the duality of mind and matter through the Magic Theater. His polarity with the Mozart consciousness heightens Haller's awareness of Mozart's transcendence.

Erica

A friend of Haller's; her picture is prominently displayed in his apartment, and she and Haller frequently quarrel.

14

The Professor

A complacent, right-wing extremist who hates Jews and Communists.

Attorney-General Loering

A visionary bureaucrat who lacks conscience and rational izes his having been responsible for men's deaths by stating that it was his duty as a public prosecutor.

Gustav

He returns to join Haller in destroying the products of the military-industrial complex. Unlike the attorney-general, he kills for pleasure.

CRITICAL COMMENTARIES

PREFACE

This section of the novel serves the important function of placing all that follows into proper perspective, and the instru ment through which this is accomplished is the retrospective first-person narrative of the landlady's nephew. We are given certain crucial pieces of information in this section which make Haller's manuscript intelligible to us. Much, of course, is left to the reader for conjecture—but we at least learn of the nephew's familiarity with Greek classicism which gives some degree of probability for his attraction to the classical ideals so embraced in Haller's recorded moments of transfiguration. Despite the nephew's middle-class milieu and seeming preoccupation with "business," he is well read and inclined toward cultural enter tainments. He comes upon Haller's manuscript by accident; he tells us about his encounters with Haller, his impression of Haller's background and tastes, and about Haller's collection of notes. And all we know about the nephew is what he tells us himself, with the exception of a few references within the manuscript.

We learn that Haller's book collection included many works from Germany's eighteenth century; and we learn, too, that Haller admired Goethe — so, we can probably assume that Haller was familiar with such philosophers of that era as Arthur Schopenhauer and Immanuel Kant. The reasons for his probable familiarity with these minds goes far beyond the mere consistency of a library, however. Schopenhauer presented his concepts of will and intellect in his *The World as Will and Idea*, and Kant is famous for what is known as the "transcendental aesthetic" in his dictum on art for art's sake in *The Critique of Pure Reason*. Harry Haller's idealism concerning artistic form, his inner division and torment relating to the collective activity or "will" of his age, and the agonizing insight of "intellect" remind us of Schopenhauer and Kant. Such clues about Haller, plus the heavily introspective quality of the nephew, help to place much of the novel in perspective. The reader, however, has to place much of it in perspective himself because a demand similar to Haller's in synthesizing is also placed upon us. We must undergo the process of synthesis as we undergo psychoanalysis ourselves with Haller. Haller, in a sense, is a martyr (the nephew calls him a "true Christian martyr") because he suffers hell and deliverance — of which we, the readers, symbolically partake. And he undergoes an exorcism of the evil of a whole segment of society in what he leaves behind; his records are his exorcism. The nephew conscientiously picks them up and prepares them for all men, particularly the more than literate middle-class intelligensia, to read and follow so that all of society may be saved.

Steppenwolf is the only instance in Hesse where we find a lengthy formal introduction in a novel, and it is his only work in which he used a contemporary setting. As previously noted, this is not a strict *roman à clef,* but the unnamed cultural metropolis is probably either Basel or Zürich.

In placing the body of the work in perspective, the indispensable prologue traces the development of a bond between

Haller and his complementary double, the landlady's nephew, who was at first skeptical and guarded toward the strangely bohemian and alien Haller. He, however, became so inextricably and fraternally bound to Haller that he had plaguing dreams and memories of him, long after Haller's ten-months stay at the house. As their acquaintance developed, we learn, the nephew grew to appreciate Haller's apparent intellectuality and, therefore, ultimately salvaged what appeared to be the genuine manuscript of a tormented potential genius, a manuscript that ordinary men would have dismissed as the aberrant scribblings of a deranged man. The nephew finds the notes to be of so much significance to men of his time that he plans to publish them.

A basic issue in this novel is a pervasive one in twentieth-century German literature: the middle-class view of illness and health in terms of the respective absence or presence of will as a life force. Intellect is frequently associated with what would seem to be illness — and yet it is these estranged beings who have the true vision of the inner sickness of the times, a sickness rooted to that very will which the Bürgers associate with the ambition and activity which amasses fortunes and builds empires.

Harry Haller, in some ways, bears a resemblance to Raskolnikov in Dostoevski's *Crime and Punishment*. Note the similarity between their untidy attic apartments; note also that each is an idealist; in addition, neither Raskolnikov nor Haller can reconcile himself with the Nietzschean vision of a world in which the powerful feel justified in unleashing their will. In addition, both Raskolnikov and Haller have a propensity toward murder, but Haller's is directed inward, against himself. His inability to attain the peace of the masters of music and poetry is rooted in the fact that his self is so divided that all he can achieve artistically are some lines of poetry and some anti-establishment newspaper articles. His divine "golden thread" which has endowed him with his responsiveness to genius is also a curse, for because of his ability to respond, he can also see his own inadequacy. Some critics might indict Haller for being a n'er-do-well who is also a fraud, but Haller seems conscious of this himself: he is sufficiently contaminated by will as to be incapable of the irduous duties of enterprise. He is not only in an individual imbo, but he is representative of a collective one as well, and s so polarized that he can calmly imagine his committing suicide.

The twentieth century will never produce a Bach, a Handel, a Mozart, or a Goethe because, according to Haller, will has so contaminated the Kantian ideal of art for art's sake that music has become the projection of a frenzied, chaotic, destructive national consciousness. The classical ideals of self-discipline—balance and simplicity in idealized form—have been crushed by the magnitude and tangled dissonance of modernity. As Haller could be called a fraud, so could all of the twentieth-century intelligensia who aspire to artistic achievement. The times that produced the Immortals is, according to Haller, gone forever.

Haller, however, is seemingly unique in that he can recognize the contaminant from which the disease ensues, and thus proceeds through a kind of self-hypnosis with a diagnosis and prognosis, which are negative unless the ego can be extinguished for the ideal. Haller is a tormented creature who hungers for the unity of pure, balanced form which emerges from pure intellect. He thrashes about with his mercurial, ever-shifting personality, his acts being frequently contradictory. He seems bohemian and yet he eagerly pays his rent in advance and complies with the rules of the house. He shrinks from the routine of notifying the local police of his new residence and yet he is magnetically drawn to the sights and smells of middle-class housekeeping.

Once the details of Haller's arrival and personal appearance are completed, focus is placed on the bond which forms between Haller and the nephew. For the latter, Haller represents the dark allurement of a world very different from that of men bound to duty and responsibility; Haller's world of literary and artistic things is considered impractical and strangely Eastern to the Bürger mentality. The nephew initially becomes so curious and taken by Haller that he goes beyond his middle-class prejudices and indulges in a bit of snooping through the stranger's apartment—before he has even been invited to Haller's apartment.

The bond between Haller and the nephew, which forms a large part of the perspective of the book, is further revealed in the prologue during the nephew's reminiscences of three specific encounters with Haller. The first of these evening encounters happened near the end of Haller's stay when he and the nephew had become rather friendly to one another. Attracted by Haller's intellectuality and sensitivity, he recalls Haller's attitude toward the pseudo-intelligensia: a withering glance, flashed in a confiding way to the nephew during a boring public lecture. The glance is memorable to the nephew for its being a signal of Haller's recognition of the triteness and shallowness of twentieth-century academe and the public's ignorance of the speaker's fraudulent, pompous tricks.

Shortly after Haller's arrival, the nephew immediately recognizes the fact that Haller is suffering from some strange malady—spleen, perhaps, but he readily senses that this is an outgrowth of Haller's superior mentality, "a profusion of gifts and powers that had not attained to harmony." These gifts and powers include his artistic idealism and intellect—irreconcilable with contemporary values. Because Haller might well have considered himself a fraud in a society of frauds, unable to embrace the ideal in a world where artistic joy is but a fleeting thing, he views himself with contempt and thus practices self-hate.

The nephew surmises that Haller was probably brought up in an austere German family; he thinks that Haller's family probably believed that individuality was wrong and that one was made to feel guilty for exhibiting marked individuality. Haller, however, was not broken. Currently, his idea of misery is the thought of his ever working in an office, a place where one feels the pressures of the competitive world of will and enterprise, and he is agonized by society's complacency in spiritual and artistic matters. We have arrived at a crucial part of the book when the nephew reflects on Haller's self-hate: ". . . self-hate is really the same thing as sheer egoism, and ultimately breeds the same cruel isolation and despair." Haller is conscious of his own hopeless exigencies and of those of the world around him. He knows that if he can attain the permanent nirvana of art, embodied in the Immortals, then this consciousness of self-limitation will disappear; likewise, he will be rid of his ego-obsessed self-hate and the frustration of feeling himself just a quasi-bourgeois fraud who indirectly aids and abets such enemies to idealism and art as Germany's right-wing establishment. The antidote for Haller's self-hate is a detachment which includes humor. As Vasudeva and the river smile and sublimely laugh for Siddhartha, so will Goethe and Mozart smile and laugh for Haller. As "OM" is Siddhartha's sacred key to self-realization and the absolving of one's ego, so Mozart enlivens Haller's intellect, his "thread of gold"; Mozart and his disciplined music, it should be noted, had much the same significance for Hesse: they represented the most perfect and eternal elements of form.

Haller's apartment contains many belongings which remind one of Hesse as well as give insight into Haller. Mention has already been made of the volumes in Haller's personal library, but we should consider other objects as well. Hesse was fascinated by southern Europe, particularly Italy, and one notices a picture of a southern landscape on Haller's wall. Hesse enjoyed water coloring as a pastime, producing numerous pastoral paintings (perhaps an influence from the East); Haller also paints water colors. Hesse was as un-Germanic in his artistic tastes as he was in his language studies, and we can see Hesse's taste reflected in Haller's interest in Italian Renaissance painting and Eastern sculpture.

Of the various encounters involving Haller which the nephew recalls, he particularly remembers their first lengthy conversation; during it, Haller revealed, despite his estrangement, his basic attraction to middle-class things. The nephew recalls their meeting one another on the stairs and he brings our attention to some poignant remarks made by Haller regarding the little household commonplaces along the stairwell and the downstairs hallway. The reason this particular section of the prologue is important is because it suggests Haller's fascination with experiences not directed by the conscious will. Such experiences have the power to transfigure a man and are frequently associated with memories of childhood. Of these sensory memories, smells seem to have a special effect on Haller, lifting him from unwilled, involuntary memory into a state of ecstasy. The fragrance of potted plants in the fastidiously polished hallway evokes a childlike, idealized vision of Bürger life, and Haller periodically tries to retrieve and expand this part of his past by sitting now and then and inhaling the smells of turpentine and flowers. He tries to recapture the original sensations of the past as the floral fragrances evoke memories of his mother. Then he invites the nephew into his apartment for the first time and reads some passages from his favorite works of literature.

The nephew recalls an evening when they separately attended a concert during which the nephew scrutinized Haller's facial reactions as Haller responded to the varied program of music; he was obviously fascinated by the disciplined neoclassical forms of Friedemann Bach, but he seemed barely to hear the somewhat dissonant modernity of "Variations and Fugue on a Theme by Mozart" by Max Reger, the controversial German composer, one of the forerunners of the more radically atonal composers of our century.

Another evening involving Haller which the nephew recalls vividly is one which seemed to mark the beginning of Haller's extreme turmoil in the latter part of his stay, the period during which he began to spend entire days in his room while he was writing his manuscript. On the particular evening in question, a woman with whom Haller had planned to spend an evening's outing arrived at the house. However, less than an hour after their departure, Haller returned alone, terribly dejected. Successive encounters between Haller and this woman ended in violent arguments and depression. One might note a parallel to Haller's distress in Hesse's own life; each had a wife who became insane. Contact with Erica might have aggravated Haller's already frayed nerves and may have triggered old memories, thus partially inducing his state of mind during the writing of the manuscript. Indeed, Haller's deeply probing manuscript is more than the mere product of marital difficulties, and already it has been pointed out that this novel is not merely a *roman à clef*, but certain incidents might bear significance as manifestations of a divided personality.

As the nephew reflects on the fantasies and quasi-fictional elements of Haller's records, he makes the keen observation that these fantasies are not mere fabrications, but are symbolically founded in the matrix of deep personal truths: ". . . the deeply lived spiritual events which he has attempted to express by giving them the form of tangible experiences." The suggestion is made by the narrator after his remarks on the manuscript that there is a possibility that Haller committed suicide, but he dismisses this idea as probably inaccurate because he feels that the manuscript served as a catharsis (or in the case of this "true Christian martyr," an exorcism) for Haller.

The nephew's final statements concerning Haller's manuscript reveal that, despite his middle-class background, he has a genuine appreciation and understanding of the manuscript. He sees it as a document of the times; he believes that Haller's "soul sickness" is not merely the aberration of a single individual, but the sickness of Haller's generation. Further, he believes that the sickness does not afflict only the weak and the worthless, but particularly those who are the strongest in spirit and richest in artistic gifts.

The manuscript, then, is an attempt to manifest schizophrenia —not just tell about it. Like the twentieth century, with its polarity of the will against the classical and literary Western heritage of intellect, the manuscript is a journey through Hell, a plunge into the abyss of the collective soul of man. The nephew then finishes by recalling that Haller told him once that every epoch has its own characteristic will, even the murky Dark Ages. Even the very worst, least enlightened epochs had their own separate identities, but the twentieth century embodies, instead, an unresolved clash of new and old: it is a terrifying age of transition in which the absolutes of the past overlap with the non-rational uncertainties of the future. The result is an irrevocable, destructive conflict. The narrator remarks that there are times when a whole generation is so caught between two epochs that two life styles emerge. The consequence is that the generation loses all power to understand itself. We are reminded that a generation earlier Friedrich Nietzsche postulated his theory of the *Übermensch* and of will as a positive force in what he regarded as a world contaminated by the slave morality of the weak. In a world where the absolutes of morality, philosophy, and religion seem to fail in answering man's great questions concerning truth, we see manifestations of the Nietzschean will and its problematical aspects in a superman-oriented, supernationalistic Germany.

"FOR MADMEN ONLY"

Haller has given his volume of memoirs a very apt title, a title bearing tremendous irony because it suggests that in order to comprehend truth, one must expand one's consciousness to a degree which the average, "normal" citizen would label insanity. According to Hesse, twentieth-century man's quest for truth cannot be resolved on rational grounds by absolutes. The deepest truths do not come by one's conscious will because most of our psyche lies in the unconscious; revelations come only in fleeting, flickering moments of unwilled spontaneity. In this segment, the reader can observe a kind of parallel between Arthur Schopenhauer's mystical conception of Nirvana (or nothingness) and Jung's conception of the collective unconscious. Nirvana and the unconscious are non-rational states, bordering on madness, according to some critics, and are important in understanding the title of Haller's records.

This section, which follows the prologue and ends just prior to the Magic Theater sequence, forms a second portion of the novel even though the work is not divided formally into chapters. It is told in relatively conventional prose and some readers might dispute the conventionality of the style because of certain unannounced departures from reality, but these are, for the most part, only occasional and the plot line is still paramount.

In the prologue, we were presented with the nephew's (possibly a potential Haller-type himself) view of Haller. In the sequence immediately preceding the treatise, we have the Steppenwolf's own interpretation of his problematical self. Basically, the Haller-type is established as a lost or misplaced bourgeois, what some people refer to as a "bourgeois manqué."

This solitary, internally polarized creature calls himself a "wolf of the steppes," the steppes being the alien domain to which such divided personalities are exiled by self and society. Haller has, voluntarily, cut himself off from those transitory things from which ordinary men derive their pleasure. These ordinary men are incapable of fathoming eternity, for they have not been endowed with the "golden thread" which would give them the capacity for insight and awareness. This golden thread is an endowment exclusive to those who appear sick by bourgeois standards. It is the anguish of unattainability which curses the artistic Steppenwolf-type; common men are spared from continual anguish because in them there is no battle between will and intellect. The bourgeois are not bothered by the twentieth century's artistic sterility; they are preoccupied by the active life of enterprise of which the will is the vital factor and time the godhead. To them, creativity is impractical, irrational, and almost malevolent because it subordinates time and interferes with duty and responsibility.

As Haller realizes how thoroughly he is rooted in the middle class, he lapses into a state bordering on psychic depression for he is aware of so much fraud within the bourgeois intelligensia. Yet he has a tender respect for the middle-class houses of his reveries while at the same time he professes abhorrence for bourgeois standards. He seems almost free as an artistic spirit, yet he is still bound to the bourgeoisie because he is dependent upon it financially and he is aesthetically stifled by it. Haller has fleeting moments of joy and release, yet too often he is bound by the time-obsessed, ego-inflated Bürger mentality, a basic twentieth-century predicament, according to Hesse, of the artist.

As Haller walks down the foggy city streets, morbidly contemplating the valuelessness of his existence, he lapses into a reverie of his youth when the mysterious Hoffmannesque atmosphere of evenings with a Gothic quality inspired him to write poetry. He reflects regretfully that the present is devoid of any sense of aesthetic awakening except upon very rare occasions. Haller misses the mundane pleasures of the will-imbued active life of the teeming bourgeoisie, but he has other pleasures: he has psychic antennae which give him the capacity to respond to things forever lost to the bourgeoisie, an ability to see "God at work." This intuitive experience grasps essences and defies the will.

Haller recalls a specific concert of "old" music—that is, Baroque music—music superior to modern music which seems embued with the spirit of the Nietzschean *Übermensch,* the orchestrated frenzy of the Germanic nationalistic ego. Haller is able to recapture the memory of this concert of Baroque music with its elegant neoclassical balance and dignity. Its golden thread lies in its purity of disciplined form, and thus its liberation from ego contamination, for classical self-discipline has almost the effect of meditation in extinguishing the aberrations of ego and idiosyncrasy. Even the sculpture of the Greeks, perhaps the very purest root of the classical tradition in art, was idealized form—not mere portraiture of passing individuals in a solid medium. The golden thread of this superb old music draws the evocation of it into an actual present and it penetrates Haller's soul.

Haller recalls other instances of direct firsthand experience with the golden thread—instances of a sublimely transcendent and yet almost torturous, transient quality. One such experience took place while he was reading poetry; another took place in the presence of his beloved. It seems that Haller's non-rationally founded, unwilled response to ultimate harmony never ceases to fascinate the nephew, despite the nephew's seeming obsession with technology and progress. It is this golden thread whose "beams" enliven Haller's intellect in a world of unchanneled will that sustains him, and it is through it that he can perceive essences beyond the ordinary world.

As Haller continues to stroll, he feels within himself a fleeting and alluring quality similar to that of the golden thread—but this time it is peculiar and bizarre. It is a vision of letters vaguely resembling an electric sign, announcing upcoming entertainments. The vision fascinates Haller because it is an involuntary experience, an experience not elicited by the conscious will; it taps the wellspring of intellect, a mental faculty beyond the reaches of ordinary men. Likewise, the entertainments themselves are not the domain of ordinary men; they are not for those whom the world thinks are "normal." These entertainments are specifically "not for everybody." This experience is the first departure from reality in the book. When Haller looks at the advertisements for the Magic Theater, the last line reads "Not for Everybody"; but when he turns to look again, the words have changed to the bizarre "For Madmen Only." Some might believe that these visions are merely a result of the various pain relievers to which Haller seems to be addicted, but their significance lies in that they serve to distinguish Haller from other men and to emphasize his fascination for that which lies submerged in the subconscious, evoked only in moments when the conscious will is suspended. Haller is fascinated by the lure of the chaotic and the dissolute; it is in his encounters with these elements that he will find the hope of resolution through exorcism.

After experiencing the mysterious letters and their eerie reflection on the black sheen of the street, Haller takes refuge in a familiar old tavern which has remained unchanged in more than a quarter of a century. Haller observes the clientele, some of which could be possible Steppenwolf-types. Contemplating the reverie-invoking atmosphere of the place, his mind wanders; a succession of forgotten piano notes returns to him, generating memories of paintings, literature, and history. All of this seemingly chaotic jumble culminates with his being reminded of the golden thread and Mozart. Hesse himself associated Mozart with the essence of beauty; Mozart's name served as a kind of cipher, signaling the onset of that ecstasy which often accompanies creative intellect. Haller is now somewhat regenerated, lifted from his feelings of suffering: "The golden trail was blazed and I was reminded of the eternal, and of Mozart, and of the stars. . . . I could breathe once more and live and face existence."

Haller continues his solitary walk down the cold, damp street. He is subsequently confronted with echoes of the antithesis of the Mozart ideal — the alluring pulse of hot, commercial jazz emanating from a cheap dance hall. This music embodies a sense of abandon and a pretense of sentiment, two elements which are musical counterparts to Nietzschean phenomena and will perversion—an artless, syncopated materialism. The sensual, rhythmic cacophony of the jazz seems to embody the forces of dehumanized will and collective negation. Nevertheless, despite Haller's scorn for its raucous brassiness, the primitive aggressiveness of jazz holds an appeal for him. Due to the middle-class standards which have been inherited by Haller, he tends at first to shy away from this forbidden music. He has not yet had the chance to experience it firsthand and must be guided into an understanding of jazz by Hermine, just as Dante was guided through Hell by Virgil. He must be able, through firsthand encounter, to observe and live through the aggregations of the fad-oriented jazz band so that he can see the seriousness of man's obsessions with such things and see the humor of it as well. Once Haller gains some objectivity and the ability to observe this musical notation of an age, then he will be able to understand the humor in it, a humor much like that which is evoked today by "pop" or "op" art.

Haller prefers the raw artlessness of this jazz, however, to contemporary academic music. He senses a pretentious dissolution in the academic tastes of the day, a sense of disease and violence which harbors the perverse forces of anarchy and annihilation. In music, this corrosive extremism is epitomized in the frantically chromatic and hugely orchestrated excesses of the interminable, unresolved melodic lines of Richard Wagner. Jazz of even the most commercial ilk is overt, according to Haller, whereas contemporary serious music embodies sinister forces, disguising rather than releasing its cryptic notation of potential eruption into chaos.

Returning to the mysterious wall, Haller looks hopefully for the mirage-like door. It is not there, but his attention is absorbed by a signbearing peddler. After being requested to allow Haller to read his placard, he turns around and Haller again sees fleeting letters reeling about in random fashion:

Anarchist Evening Entertainment
Magic Theater
Entrance Not For Everybody

Haller is intensely fascinated by this almost hallucinogenic vision, for it promises a reality beyond will or phenomena. Upon Haller's inquiry about these "entertainments," the peddler begins to walk wearily away and, upon Haller's pursuit, gives Haller a little booklet and disappears.

Overwrought with fatigue and arriving back at his landlady's house, Haller draws out the little book to examine it. He sees to his astonishment that is a treatise on the Steppenwolf. As we read through this next section, much of the material about Haller's multiple personality will be reviewed for us. But the treatise is important because it helps explain further Haller's golden thread. Past ages which are forever lost chronologically become, for exhilarating, fleeting moments, an essential reality which transcends time and defies rational analysis. Even though the classical age of Mozart and Goethe has chronologically gone by, its divine presence — through its music — suspends time and affirms a kind of life beyond the temporal realm.

TREATISE ON THE STEPPENWOLF

Before actually reading the treatise, some readers might expect it to be somewhat dull due to its length and its essay form, which departs from the novel's narrative. It may also come a little unexpectedly, although several distinguished modern novelists (Proust, Joyce, Mann) dealing with the predicament of the artist allow analytical essays to appear in their works. The essay vaguely resembles a Pietist tract, bringing an element of mysticism to the material on the Steppenwolf's inspirations and self-realization. Some translators use the word "tractate" instead of "treatise" due to its closeness to *tractat* in the original German. Hesse was familiar with such tracts because his father's Calw publishing house circulated many of them for missionaries and their converts.

Basically, the treatise postulates and elaborates upon two types of Steppenwolves. This is done because a Steppenwolf is so precariously balanced between two worlds that he may go in either direction — the direction of will or the direction of intellect. A Steppenwolf is a man whose rare talents and vision set him apart from everyday people. If he veers toward will, a Steppenwolf could become a great entrepreneur, inventor, or engineer. However, if he veers toward intellect, a Steppenwolf is not so fortunate because pure art is impossible in our time and the Steppenwolf's life will never be fulfilled. The will-Steppenwolf can respond to flux and change and make his mission one for progress. Yet because he does not hover midway in torment, he is not a true Steppenwolf in the sense that Haller is one.

Harry Haller is a Steppenwolf in the truest sense, and any fulfillment that comes within his reach is only fleeting, the lot of artist types. There is also a dichotomy of God/Satanism which plagues the artist's soul — a postulation reminiscent of that made by the French poet Charles Baudelaire. Nevertheless, despite the artist-Steppenwolf's doom to intense torment, he is endowed with a capacity for intense joy beyond the furthest reaches of the world of phenomena. An artist on a par with the Immortals could, likewise, transmit this joy to others through the radiant permanence of his creations. Even though an artist-Steppenwolf cannot attain to pure intellect because of the vast will-contamination by the twentieth century, vestiges of intellect yet untrammeled by will give such an individual the ability to apprehend permanence and eternity.

Among the artist-Steppenwolf's strange ways are his solitary nocturnal walks and his propensity toward suicide. At the root of the latter is his ego, ". . . an extremely dangerous, dubious and doomed germ of nature." This concern for the negative qualities of the ego is part of the Jungian influence which implies that the ego is a projection of the corrupt "anima" (associated with *Natur)* of the personality. The influence of Arthur Schopenhauer is present, also, in the references to individuation and its association with guilt. Much of Schopenhauer's material on individuation is drawn from the Eastern mystics' concept of the transmigration of souls. This cycle of reincarnative birth-death, or metempsychosis is directly related to the ordeal of sansara (associated with dissolution, guilt, and chaos) through which one must pass to return to Asia, the Eternal Mother, the beginning of things. Nirvana, the Eastern concept of salvation, is the converse of individuation — a depersonalizing process involving a psychic *tabula rasa* on which eternal essences can be imprinted. Cultures, according to this theory, must also undergo this process. The dissolution and demise of one culture gives rise to the beginning of a new culture. Hesse's idea of a new culture, a pure culture in which there are no wars and where a perfect synthesis of will and intellect exists, is explored in a utopian novel set in the twenty-fourth century, *The Glass Bead Game (Magister Ludi)*, for which the author won the Nobel Prize in 1946.

The treatise which Haller reads is suffused with mysticism and, we realize, has strong echoes of *Siddhartha*. For example, consider the section of *Siddhartha* in which the protagonist has just left the city, obsessed with the transitory quality of the illusion-filled life style and hanging on the precipice of suicide: ". . . suicides present themselves as those who are overtaken by the sense of guilt inherent in individuals, those souls that find the aim of life not in the perfecting and molding of the self, but in liberating themselves by going back to the mother, back to God, back to the all." This is basically what is involved in Nirvana, the extinguishing or surrendering of the ego. The treatise concludes its remarks on suicide by deprecating the act as shabby; suicide displays the most extreme sort of ego for it is an act of will. Suicide affirms the supremacy of will and the surrender to the chaotic, dissolute forces of negation. Man can overcome this world of illusory phenomena not by suicide but by meditation, an ascendency of intellect which apprehends eternity — suspending time, affirming life, and denying death. Albert Camus was to write in "The Myth of Sisyphus" in 1943, sixteen years after *Steppenwolf*: "It is nobler and finer to be conquered by life than to fall by one's own hand."

The treatise then examines Haller's relationship with the bourgeoisie, a class to which he seems alien and yet to which he is magnetically drawn. He does not wish to envisage himself as a system-man, and yet, to a large extent, he is one. Some might think of this haunting man-wolf creature as a kind of semi-animal, but he has qualities that are more human than most people. It is his outward appearance which repulses middle-class men (as does Gregor Samsa's changed appearance in Kafka's "The Metamorphosis"). Within Haller are standards of decency as high as those of any middle-class man. In fact, he abhors any crime of violence more than ordinary men because of his intellect's hyperconsciousness of respectable society's war-mongering super-patriotism.

As the excursus on the bourgeoisie continues, the men of this class are described as people who avoid conspicuous, readily observable extremes, but who, in a more sinister way, embrace the most extreme of extremes — that is, they place the will above all else. Steppenwolves, in contrast, have a sense that makes them superior to the majority of sheep-like people. If the Steppenwolf's ability to project and if his extraordinary spirit are channeled into personal drive and ambition, he becomes a will-Steppenwolf who contributes to the system and strengthens it. These men stand out from ordinary men because of their individuality. In the artist-Steppenwolf, intellect holds the will in check, and the introspective man becomes aware of the guilt inherent in individuation. He cannot reconcile himself to the change and flux of our times in which the will thrives. Because the contrast in the artist-Steppenwolf's personality is so pronounced, he is conscious "that all extreme individuation turns against itself intent upon its own destruction." He devotes his life to meditation of pure essence although the creation of original, pure art is fruitless in the twentieth century. He aspires to the realm of the Immortals rather than to personal success. Those other Steppenwolves who remain in the ambitious circles of the middle class devote their gifts to technical progress, wealth, and national security. Yet there is also hope for these will-Steppenwolf men through humor.

Even though he may submerge himself in his work, a Steppenwolf is never really depolarized. But as the Immortals can temporarily extinguish polarity in the artist type, humor holds hope for the type in which will is dominant. This "kingdom of humor" is central to the novel because artist types can find it also, upon visitation by the Immortals. Even though this humor is somewhat bourgeois in quality, the bourgeois do not really understand it. For instance, a bourgeois of today with no problematical Steppenwolfian quality would not understand what is humorous in large posters of Coke bottles and Campbell soup cans. Only Steppenwolves can grasp the ultimate comedy and affirmation inherent in cosmic humor, and it is this which depolarizes them. Humor is central to the novel because it resembles meditation; inherent in humor is the observing and resolving of chaos by rising above it, and the subsequent detachment from it through the transcendence of inner synthesis. This meditative process requires self-examination; one "must look deeply into the chaos of one's soul and plumb its depths."

A sequence occurs which prefigures the end of the book, with the references to mirrors and Haller's impending self-examination. The split personality of the precariously balanced man-wolf will either explode and completely scatter, or it will "come to terms in the dawning light of humor." Inherent in the process of synthesis and the cosmic vision is an ability to see objectively all levels of the world and of consciousness, as in a looking glass.

The treatise continues to its conclusion with an explanation that the Steppenwolf's self is not split into only two parts but into a thousand fragments, and that the oscillations of his life are likewise between thousands of poles. Thus, to regard the thousandfold chaos of the ego as twofold is a delusion. Some of the material that follows at this point is again reminiscent of *Siddhartha*. The comment is made that the ancient poets of India did not deal with the individual ego or the individual hero, but dealt instead with "whole reels of individualities in a series of incarnations." Likewise, in modern poetry, poets (artist-Steppenwolves) deal with the "manifold activity of soul" and with their characters as "the various facets and aspects of a higher unity . . . of the poet's soul." Hesse alludes to Faust, suggesting that he, like the Steppenwolf, is imbued with the delusion of the twofold personality. Man, to attain inner harmony and peace, must confront the illusion of a single, unified personality. Here one can observe a Jungian influence, and a contrast between the West and the East ensues. Hesse admired the wisdom and sense of permanence of the East and considered the West's progress-oriented influence as a corruption and a defilement.

The ability to strip one's ego bare, to surrender the ego (as taught in the East) brings immortality. Mozart, Haller's favorite of the Immortals, attained his immortality by transcending his sansara-like existence and attaining the essence of form by his immense powers of "surrender and suffering." The process of surrendering the ego and of subsequent synthesis is likened to a kind of Nirvana. One cannot regain lost innocence and hope to become once again as a little child by attempting to go backward chronologically or through psychic regressions. Synthesis can be attained only by passing forward first through the realm of chaos. Rather than attempting to narrow and simplify the soul, men must draw in the whole world and go through the painful ordeal of expanding the soul. One should consider the Buddhist method of attempting to escape all that is imbued with birth and subsequent time and death; as the Buddhist attempts to escape Maya, the realm of illusion, through meditation, likewise the Steppenwolf must give himself to "expansion of the soul until it is able once more to embrace the All."

Like Haller's solitary reflections, the Treatise on the Steppenwolf is a mirror of all those men who are caught in the delicate balance between going the way of will or the way of intellect. These men are the Steppenwolves of whom the Steppenwolf-Haller is but one who goes falteringly in the direction of intellect.

CONTINUATION OF HALLER'S RECORDS

Following the Treatise on the Steppenwolf comes its poetic counterpart, a poem that Haller has written (actually one of

Hesse's *Crisis* poems). This section pursues Haller's "asceticism of the intellect" and his concern with death, bringing the predicament back to Haller's wife's insanity and the job he lost. Haller feels that he cannot avoid his self-destruction from his multiple personality "unless molten in the fire of a renewed self-knowledge, he underwent a change and passed over to a self, new and undisguised."

On the raw wintry morning following the encounter with the peddler, Haller goes to bed, firm in his resolve to eventually do himself in. He reads and rereads the treatise, as well as constantly recalling the memory of the churchyard wall, realizing that the two are strangely interconnected. The announcement of the Magic Theater entertainment, with its fleeting, illuminated letters, marks the first significant departure from reality; it "promised much that was hinted at in the treatise, and the voices of that strange world aroused my curiosity."

When Haller returns to the site of the announcement, he discovers a funeral procession. The cemetery seems steamlined and gadgety, and the whole funeral sequence reeks with the odor of depersonalized modernity and efficiency. The ceremony seems to be a hollow performance, embodying a sterile, death-like hypocrisy. It even seems, in a macabre way, comic because of its "vultures" and "functionaries." Haller suddenly sees someone whom he thinks he recognizes; it is the peddler, but he is of little help. Haller is told to go to the Black Eagle.

Now Haller is at an all-time low, almost paralyzed with emptiness and despair; and, despite his disgust for the professor's sense of self-importance, he is actually pleased to come across an acquaintance. Haller accepts the professor's dinner invitation, contemplating with reservations the required courtesy and small talk. At home before the dinner, Haller reads some of his beloved eighteenth-century literature; later, while he is shaving, his thoughts return to the funeral sequence. He contemplates modern civilization in terms of the symbolic cemetery, "a cemetery where Jesus Christ and Socrates, Mozart and Haydn, Dante and Goethe were but the indecipherable names on

moldering stones." Whether or not Haller's cutting himself with
the razor is entirely coincidental is a matter for the reader's reflection for Haller is deeply depressed, has contemplated suicide
and, in his state of depression, the thought of visiting the professor becomes almost unbearable. The professor is pretentious,
self-satisfied, and naive, besides being a rabid supporter of right-
wing causes.

From the first moments after Haller's arrival at the professor's house to the visit's abrupt ending, all goes completely
wrong. Immediately upon arrival, Haller's glance falls upon a
sentimentalized etching of Goethe which is so unlike Goethe
that it seems to "shriek" at Haller (Franz Kafka made the shriek
a stock motif). In the engraving, Goethe looks more like a
bourgeois "success" than a tempermental artist. This incident of
the engraving embodies Haller's own crisis, the conflict of his
"selves." Haller's antagonism is no doubt aggravated by his
consciousness of his own Bürger background.

When the professor rails interminably about the journalist
Haller, whom he ironically alludes to as his guest's namesake
and calls him a traitor, we should realize that this is similar to
the type of reviling Hesse himself received for his articles and
columns during World War I. His writings were also blacklisted
in 1943 by the Third Reich. Like Hesse himself, Haller is conscious of Germany's war guilt, is critical of the Kaiser and other
leaders, but is not anti-German. He is merely critical of the direction his country has taken in the twentieth century. We can
almost hear Hesse himself as Haller discloses that he is the
Harry Haller who wrote the article, terminating his visit with a
declaration that "it would be better for our country and the world
in general, if at least the few people who were capable of thought
stood for reason and the love of peace instead of heading wildly
with a blind obsession for a new war."

After the visit with the professor, Haller resolves to commit
suicide, but he first takes to the streets. Despite his resolve to
return to his room, he dreads going back and so he roams the
streets for hours. He finally finds his way to the Black Eagle in

an unfamiliar part of the city. Here he will meet Hermine, who will alternately draw forth all of Haller's levels of consciousness.

Haller's encounter with Hermine marks the beginning of an apprenticeship sequence (similar to Goethe's *Wilhelm Meister*). Hermine tells Haller that, even though he is an intellectual, he has a great deal to learn — specifically, the simple pleasures of life, such as ballroom dancing, which she offers to teach him. He tells her of his life and of his experience in the professor's house, and she listens. She suggests to him that she has a special role in his life similar to that of a looking glass. She then gives him advice which is similar to that in the treatise: "If you had sense, you would laugh at the artist and the professor — laugh and be done with it." At this point, Hermine is rather like an Oedipal mother figure as she implores Haller to close his eyes and get some sleep; as he does her bidding, he closes his eyes as a child with its mother. His dream of Goethe is significant because Hesse is departing again from reality.

Haller's dream begins in a vestibule of Goethe's house where Haller has been waiting for an interview with the master. Here, a symbol with deep mythological roots as an archetype appears. It is a scorpion, noted for its strange beauty as well as for its ferocious sting. As a Jungian archetype, it symbolizes characteristics associated with women. This particular scorpion has been attempting to crawl up Haller's leg, and he has feared to reach for it. Allusion is made to the tempestuous German "Storm and Stress" poet Gottfried August Bürger (1747-94) who addressed lyric poems to a seductive mistress named Molly. Haller seems aware that there is some kind of connection between the scorpion and Molly. Then, as he considers the possibility of its being some kind of messenger from Molly, he thinks simultaneously that its name might be Vulpius. Christiane Vulpius (1765-1816) was the wife of Goethe who was, at one time, his mistress, and the name "Vulpius" relates the mythical symbol and the allurements of women.

When Goethe appears, he resembles the pretentious bourgeois of the professor's engraving rather than the artist-poet that

Haller has always envisioned. After considerable altercation, Goethe alludes to Mozart's *Magic Flute*, suggesting that it "preaches optimism and faith." Haller professes his love for *The Magic Flute* and for Mozart, its composer, asserting that, unlike Goethe, Mozart did not live to see his works regarded as monuments of creativity.

The dream image of the eighty-two-year-old Goethe tells of his conquest of life over death and, when he does so, he loses his pompous appearance and begins to bear a sublime resemblance to Mozart. The air fills itself with songs of Goethe, Mozart, and Schubert. Then Goethe reiterates the central theme of the book, as do the treatise and Hermine: "You take old Goethe much too seriously . . . we Immortals do not like things to be taken seriously. We like joking. Seriousness . . . is an accident of time. . . . In eternity, however, there is no time; eternity is a mere moment, just long enough for a joke." Goethe has even learned to dance, avoiding the obsessive idealism which has been Haller's problem. Haller asks if Molly is there, and Goethe gleefully hands Haller a jewel box containing a miniature lady's leg. This little replica becomes suddenly associated with the scorpion for, as Haller reaches for it, it seems fearfully animated. The dream ends chillingly with an aged Goethe laughing.

After the dream, Hermine tells him that she has had the same discouraging experience with saints' pictures as Haller had with Goethe's. Hermine subsequently becomes philosophical in her remarks, unusual for women of her calling. When asked if she is religious, she replies that one must be released from the concept and the demands of time and money before one can become truly religious — and this has not happened to her yet. She repeats one of the main themes of the novel: "You can't be religious in earnest and at the same time live in actual things and still take them seriously, time and money . . . and all that."

Haller's conversation with his "alter ego" has brought him to a euphoric state of relaxation. He falls asleep fully dressed and awakens several hours later refreshed and, soon after, we have a highly poignant (and often under-emphasized) conversation between Haller and his landlady. Haller's inhibitions have lifted and the time is perfect for a friendly, jocular conversation. The aunt prepares tea and, as they converse, she learns much about the normally taciturn Haller, without actually posing personal questions. She is not shocked by Haller's nocturnal absence; in fact, she finds her tenant's solitary, quiet ways agreeable. The conversation turns to the nephew and, for the first time, we are told about him from Haller's point of view. The nephew's hobby is tinkering with radios, and Haller is able to joke about this. This develops into a conversation of rare depth as Haller reflects on the nephew's fascination with scientific accomplishments. He comments that even the greatest scientific minds of the contemporary West have not grasped what the sages of India knew in ancient times — that is, the "omnipresence of all forces and facts." The wisdom of the East is permanent; the wisdom of the West is transitory. The ancients of the East were aware of the "unreality of time," which science has not yet comprehended. Haller, however, suggests that, one day, the past will be able to be retrieved and transmitted like the electronic impulses of a broadcast. Not only does the present float around us, but the past does also: "All that ever happened in the past could be recorded and played back likewise." This entire conversation proves that Haller has learned something from the dream rendezvous with Goethe; he can laugh at the impermanence embodied in the nephew's toy. The radio motif will be reintroduced near the end of the novel in the "radio music of life" sequence that includes a portrait of Mozart, laughing.

Anticipating his dinner date with Hermine, Haller reveals the positive effect she has had on him: "What I longed for in my despair was life and resolution, action and reaction, impulse and impetus." Later that evening, Hermine will become, in Jungian terms, Haller's "anima" or "shadow" in the form of a sexually ambiguous hermaphrodite. She vaguely reminds Harry of an old-time school friend named Hermann, and the composite of masculine/feminine can be easily observed in the names Hermann/Hermine. We also know that "Harry" is a diminutive of "Hermann," and so the observation can also be made that

Harry/Hermann/Hermine are one composite personality. (The sequence involving the reminiscence of a boyhood friend in a woman's presence is akin to Castorp's recollection of the sexually ambiguous Pribislav Hippe in Clavdia Chauchat's presence in Thomas Mann's *Magic Mountain.*) The idea of the female "anima" here symbolizes the inclination toward dissolution and corruption inherent in *Natur;* the male "animus" symbolizes the realms of the mind and spirit inherent in *Geist.* It is at this point of self-recognition that Haller guesses Hermine's name.

The nucleus of the Haller-Hermine relationship is further solidified when she tells Haller of her role as a mirror: ". . . the reason why I please you and mean so much to you is because I am a kind of looking glass for you, because there's something in me that answers you and understands you." Haller is quite correct when he answers that she is his opposite, that she has all he lacks. Shortly afterward, a premonition of a future departure from reality ensues when Hermine indicates that Haller will carry out certain orders, that he will carry out her command and kill her. This prefigures Haller's "killing" his "other self" embodied in the image of Hermine in the picture world of Pablo's Magic Theater. This often misunderstood event symbolizes the only partially successful attempt at extinguishing Haller's conscious ego and his necessity for attaining the undestructive, gleeful perception of the Immortals.

Events proceed rapidly now: the following day, Haller finds Hermine curiously looking at a right-wing newspaper containing excoriating references to Haller as "a noxious insect and a man who disowned his native land." Haller is, above all, disturbed by the prospect of another war, "the next war that draws nearer and nearer, and it will be a good deal more horrible than the last." After several pages of anti-war material, Hermine takes Harry, as it were, under her wing. They purchase a record player, take it to Harry's apartment, and practice the fox trot. On the following day, Harry is to dance in public for the first time. Here Haller is introduced to Pablo, for whom he instantly feels the antagonism of jealousy in Hermine's presence—not a lover's jealousy, Haller says, but a "subtler jealousy." Haller is also antagonistic toward Pablo because he is the polar opposite of Mozart, Haller's idol.

Hesse is readying us for this transformation: Haller will have to undergo the process of expanding his soul, and he will have to reconcile himself with the jazz world in order to effect "the disintegration of the personality"; this will be a painful process. Currently, Haller is undergoing deep self-examination under the tutelage of Hermine; he is "given over bit by bit to self-criticism and at every point is found wanting." His Bürger beliefs are no longer strong. He, nevertheless, still has reservations about what he considers "slumming" in dance halls, and his opinion of Pablo is still negative. We learn in this section of Pablo's drug habits and what he thinks about music. For Pablo, music is an immediate, nonverbal experience; for Haller, music is a spiritually transcendent and thereby permanent experience.

Much inner turmoil ensues; suffering and happiness come simultaneously — as, for example, when Haller finds Maria in his room after an organ recital of Buxtehude, Pachelbel, Bach, and Haydn, which induced reveries of the past. Here is Hesse's literary counterpart of atonality. The reader is wrenched from one stratum to another — from the realm of religious music to the realm of Maria. During a walk immediately following the recital, Haller comes to the realization that much of Germany's heritage has rested in the irrational emotionality of its music (the collective "anima" or *Natur* of the collective German personality). Rather than turning to the mind or reason (*Geist*) in which he (and Hesse) have faith, Germany is turning to dissolution, to dreams of a "speech without words that utters the inexpressible and gives form to the formless." This embodies the chaos, the process of decadence and decay, elements that were never "passed home to reality."

According to Hesse, modern music (from Brahms and culminating in Wagner), with its spirit of anarchy, will ultimately give way to the corroded irrationality that is but a hair's breadth from the Nazi mystique. It is this state of confusion that is lessened upon encountering Maria, who has been sent by

Hermine. Maria is a variation on the character of Kamala in *Siddhartha*, teaching the art of love to the intellectual ascetic.

On the following day, Haller finds out that he is to participate in the upcoming Fancy Dress Ball, a kind of masked ball that serves as Hesse's counterpart to Goethe's Walpurgis Nacht sequence in *Faust*. After a series of reflections and musings on love, Haller encounters all three members of the offbeat coterie, learning of and rejecting many of their weird secrets. He finds Maria in many ways a joy, but he finds Pablo's amorality repugnant. Ambiguity of gender is repeated in Hermine's oblique references to her relationship with Maria.

Preceding the Fancy Dress Ball, a feeling of heavy anticipation prevails. Hermine is to become a kind of Mephistopheles, and the sequence begins with Haller's remark that what he is looking for is not ordinary happiness or contentment, but a kind of "spiritual food." Haller is cognizant of the fact that sensual pleasures do not last. As in Cervantes' *Don Quixote*, Haller's quest here is for the unattainable, and he feels disenchanted because of the immense gulf between the ideal and the real. At this point, Hermine makes a remark that is memorable for its philosophical depth: "Time and the world, money and power belong to the small people, the shallow people. To the rest, the real men, belongs nothing . . . but death" and "eternity . . . the kingdom on the other side of time and appearances . . . for that reason . . . we long for death." This is what the Immortals (Steppenwolf-types who have attained equilibrium) live for. Here Hermine transcends her profession and reminds us of Socrates in Plato's *Phaedo*, in which the true philosopher is presented as the man who tends his soul, cultivating his awareness of reality by engaging in a constant process of dying (attaining "ideals," "forms," or "essences"). Like Plato's philosopher, Hesse's Immortals live for eternity. Hermine also suggests that, among the saints, many were sinners first. She remarks that we must err "before we reach home. And we have no one to guide us. Our only guide is our homesickness." Hermine's comments about spiritual rebirth remind us of Sonya's remarks in *Crime and Punishment* concerning the miracle of Lazarus. When Haller leaves, he becomes ever more conscious of the similiarity between his mind and Hermine's — that her mind is but a side of his and that her thoughts are his also.

Hermine does more than just teach Haller to dance; she has recovered for him "the sacred sense of beyond, of timelessness, of a world which had an eternal value and the substance of which was divine." The dream of Goethe laughing returns to Haller and he feels for the first time that he understands it. The laughter is light and clear; it penetrates eternity and time and it includes a return to innocence.

The philosophical dialogue with Hermine remains in Haller's mind for a long time; even as he goes to meet Maria once again, he continues to reflect on the Immortals "living their life in timeless space." His mind settles around compositions of Bach and Mozart, whose artistic permanence suspends time, giving a feeling of time frozen in space. Suddenly Haller hears the laughter of the Immortals and he hurriedly writes down a poem ("The Immortals"). Later, however, his mood changes when he becomes conscious of a dread of death — a dread, however, that is already conscious of its being a surrender and a release.

The final section of *Steppenwolf*, which includes the Magic Theater sequence, begins with the events leading up to and including the Masked Ball. Haller has taken leave of Maria and has slept; upon awakening, he suddenly remembers the festivities of the upcoming evening while shaving. No doubt, the fact that Haller is shaving and looking in a mirror is significant because he is soon to be directed toward self-recognition. On his way to the ball, Haller stops at the Steel Helmet, well-remembered and unchanged for twenty-five years, and he has reveries of the pain and beauty of the past. He then lapses into visions of modern man, with his predilection for automobiles and war. Haller's being in a nearly dreamlike state is the author's way of preparing us for the interlude of unreality which follows shortly. On the way to the Globe Rooms, where the Masked Ball is to be held, Haller sees part of a film extravaganza of the Old Testament in which Moses resembles portraits of the rugged, white-bearded Walt Whitman. Another level shift takes place when Haller is reminded of some G. F. Handel vocal music (probably the English language oratorio of 1738, *Israel in Egypt*).

When Haller arrives at the ball, the motif of the cloakroom is introduced and much is made of the care with which Haller puts away his claim ticket. In a short while, he will not be able to find the ticket and, when given one, he will observe bizarre lettering on it much like that on the churchyard wall. Also, Haller will be instructed by Pablo, upon entering the Magic Theater, to leave his personality in the cloakroom. Now, however, we notice that Haller joins the members of the party; he enters a basement decorated much like Dante's Hell, through which he must make an ultimate ascent. The ascent is to approximate structurally the stages of Haller's process of synthesis wherein the mundane and the spiritual levels of consciousness are resolved. During the ball, Haller must surrender his conscious ego and take the (inward) path to attain the perception of the Immortals, a fine madness attainable by artists only. The admission fee is his supposedly rational, bourgeois, ego-oriented "mind."

When Haller thrusts himself back toward the basement labeled "Hell," he recognizes Maria, who tells him that Hermine is in "Hell" and that she has summoned her. When Haller sees Hermine, she is again in ambiguous clothing and resembles Harry's former school friend, Hermann. She is, seemingly, a hermaphrodite. She dances with girls, but other things are odd too: "Everything was fanciful and symbolic." At this point, as Haller lapses into a kind of incipient stupor, we are presented with one of the most important symbols in this novel—that is, Jung's idea of equilibrium and the ancient Hindu and Buddhist archetypal symbol of the All, the symbol of the lotus blossom. Dr. Jung's symbol of self-recognition was that of the mandala, the four-petaled lotus flower, and it is for this reason that we can assume that Hesse intended for the rest of the novel to contain many ideas of Jungian psychoanalysis. In antiquity, the lotus, a a symbol of the *Upanishads*, was within the heart, wherein abided Brahman or All. To know Brahman, however, one must experience the "Tat Twam Asi" (That Art Thou), Brahma dwelling within the lotus of the heart. Only in this way can man escape sorrow and death and become one with the essence of the All. Hesse and Jung were both exponents of Eastern mysticism, and, in his own way, Haller approaches a kind of Nirvana in nearly achieving unity with the Immortals. The Magic Theater sequence could be stated as being symbolic psychoanalysis in offbeat garb. The camaraderie of Pablo and Hermine represents archetypes of Haller's consciousness. At the advent of the Magic Theater sequence, Haller contemplates a peculiar bond with Pablo's psyche: "Was it not perhaps I who made him speak, who spoke from within him?"

The stimulation and excitement of the Masked Ball increases to near delirium; Haller speaks of "the intoxication of a general festivity, the mysterious merging of the personality in the mass, the mystic union of joy." The potential for overcoming inhibitions is suggested, an essential element of psychoanalysis. Images begin to liquify, much like the images in Siddhartha's river, reminding us of the primal sea; Haller says that his personality was dissolved in the intoxication of the festivity like salt in water. His exhilaration reaches new heights as he reflects on his feeling of release and on his loss of the sense of time.

As Haller has many selves, his "other self" likewise has many selves. Hermine disappears from his sight and reappears as a Pierrette whom he is to recognize as part of his other self. The feverish pace of the ball accelerates and culminates with Haller's meeting Pablo as the place resounds with music. Haller hears a superhuman laugh and Pablo invites him to a realm beyond time, for madmen only, for the price of his mind. Harry is escorted upstairs, making an ascent, to "a stratum of reality . . . rarefied in the extreme." As he mounts this staircase, symbolically to the cosmic realm, possible resolution is hinted at.

Pablo now assumes the role of a guru for Haller. He reveals that Haller has a longing to forsake this world and to penetrate a reality more native to him—a world beyond time. Pablo tells Haller that it is his soul that he seeks, but that only within exists "that other reality" for which he longs. The object of the upcoming voyage is to externalize Haller's fantasies. This "trip," to use the modern vernacular, is partially initiated by drugs, but it is important to bear in mind, drugs notwithstanding, that this expansion is only a yielding of what is already within the subject's soul. Haller has already had a pondering, idealistic mentality marred by psychic hyperactivity.

The structurally and psychologically significant mirror motif reaches its culmination as Pablo shows Haller a hand mirror; within, Haller sees the frightened eyes of a Steppenwolf. The journey then begins and Haller finds himself in a corridor full of doors, significant already as symbols. Earlier, Hermine had been thought of as a "door," and it is through opening the doors that Haller will be projected into externalized fantasy. Motifs previously introduced in the novel are also recapitulated here. Jungian psychoanalysis is presented here in a strange guise, but its essence of negating the ego is, nevertheless, present. The guru Pablo announces that what Haller wants is to be relieved of his so-called "personality" which is to be left in the cloakroom. He also suggests that the aim of the Theater is to teach Haller how to laugh, remarking that true humor begins when one ceases to take himself seriously. Much of this, of course, echoes the ideas of the Goethe dream and Hermine's remarks about it. More significantly, this is the final enactment of the treatise. This is another departure from ordinary reality. Haller is to cast aside the "spectacles" of his conscious ego, his projected self-image. He stands now before a full-length mirror which is evidently faceted, for he is apparently to see his reflection when it "fell to pieces." Here, he is prepared for catching a glimpse into the chaos of the schizophrenic soul of modern man. All sorts of Haller-creatures run helter-skelter, one young boy figure emerging running toward a door labeled "All Girls Are Yours. One Quarter in the Slot." The imaginary figure then appears to fall headfirst into the slot, and Pablo at once disappears, leaving Haller to his own resources.

At this point, the radically surrealistic Magic Theater sequence begins. It serves the dual function of being both a recapitulation of previously introduced leitmotifs and as an exorcism recounted in semi-retrospect in Haller's diary. Like the cubist painter or the atonic composer, the surrealistic novelist dissects his subject into a myriad of chaotic pieces and hints that its inner reality may be grasped through synthesis into a new harmonious whole. We might refer to the recounting of the Magic Theater as being in "semi-retrospect" because the material at the end of Haller's abandoned manuscript was probably written about the same time he left it behind. His leaving no doubt resulted from his being able to approach self-recognition because of these recollections and his synthesizing of experiences.

As far as the Magic Theater sequence is concerned, it is more valuable to be able to examine its symbols and images in terms of Jung's analytical psychology than it is to attempt to summarize it. Basically, the Magic Theater marks the culmination of Hermine's and Pablo's efforts at breaking down the ingrained inhibitions and suppressed aggressions of the man-wolf. Hermine and Pablo have been gradually eliciting complementary parts of Haller's personality; in the upcoming fantasies, they are integral parts (along with Pablo's polar opposite, Mozart) of Haller's personality. More significantly, the fantasies represent the schizophrenic selves within collective man, all of whose parts are seemingly irreconcilable and mutually exclusive. Through Harry Haller's expanded consciousness, we look closely at that sickness of the times that the nephew alluded to in the prologue.

That Haller's neurosis is more Jungian than Freudian is evident because Haller's symptoms include marital strife, domestic dislocation, the war, and a general sense of disenchantment rather than the problem of sexuality *rooted in childhood*. The Magic Theater is therapeutic because its function is to draw the symbolism of dream visions and fantasies to the surface so that the psychic forces of the deepest levels of the unconscious may be examined and constructively integrated within the conscious through a synthesizing process. Because Jungian psychoanalysis is forward-oriented rather than oriented backwards around root causes, self-recognition becomes its aim as a constructive goal.

In resolving the individual personal consciousness or ego with the collective unconscious, man's conscious self may complement his ancestral soul. For Haller, the artist's collective ancestral soul is suffused in that beatific laughter that peals at the pettiness of ego consciousness, and Haller's "trip" comes very close to being disastrous because his jealousy allows him to become deadly serious and desecrate his vision of Hermine and Pablo together. Hermine represents the mundane, illusory side of Haller's self which he unfortunately cannot view with enough classical detachment to laugh off, as Mozart might. The paranoic side of Haller's ego is shown by the bizarre mutation of the chess pieces into the form of a knife which he will use in "killing" the image of his alter ego. By not fully attaining the perception of the Immortals, and by not being able to laugh spontaneously, he stains the "stage" of his soul with blood, and he checkmates himself in the dark corner of his neurosis. His contact with that fine madness of Mozart and Goethe is caught only in fleeting moments when touched either by the golden thread or by Baroque and Classical music.

Regarding certain specifics of the Magic Theater itself, Haller has found himself in a corridor full of doors beyond which various parts of the twentieth-century personality may be examined psychoanalytically as, as it were, mental sideshows. Of the numerous choices, Haller enters only five, by which the following announcements appear:

"Jolly Hunting—Great Hunt in Automobiles"
"Guidance in the Building Up of the Personality"
"Marvelous Training of the Steppenwolf"
"All Girls Are Yours"
"How One Kills for Love"

The first of the sideshows is perhaps the most interesting because it depicts a violent enactment of inner hostilities and aggressions while impugning the contemporary military-industrial "machine complex." The paramount element of this sideshow is the "war between men and machines," of which the machines not only include cars but also political "machine-like" bureaucrats. Men are the victims of these runaway machines which pollute the air with anarchy. Haller reflects that this war, despite its ferocity, lacks real direction and that this is one of the most terrifying things about it ("Everyone . . . strove to prepare the way for a general destruction of this iron-cast civilization of ours."). In a way, it depicts the fall of Western man, and Haller joins in, hurling all his suppressed violence against the machine-oriented establishment.

Of prime importance in this section is the symbolism of the wheels of the upturned bureaucrat's car. The wheel is an archetypal symbol dating back beyond early Hindu and Buddhist symbolism. In Eastern mythology through Hinduism and Buddhism, it generally represents the realm of Maya which is associated with illusion and spiritual death. Also important is the fact that the car, an upturned wreck with its wheels wildly spinning in the air, is a Ford—the very embodiment of mass production. As Haller and Gustav examine the wreckage, allusion is made to the "Tat Twam Asi" of the Hindu *Chandogya-Upanishad* which concerns itself with the nature and subjective analysis of the self. The innermost being of universal nature, Brahman, and our innermost self, Atman, are one—"That Art Thou" (Tat Twam Asi).

The car containing Attorney-General Loering, the unquestioning public prosecutor, appears and is subsequently prevailed upon. Loering is a man of duty who justifies his role of passing sentences upon unfortunates by stating that it is his duty. In this sense, he resembles Kafka's legal bureaucrats who are oblivious to the sinister forces they represent. Significantly, Haller reflects that what seems to be the best rational order can lead to the worst oppression of all, and that war will end only if men can become more like the artist and the madman, and less like the machine-made article.

As Haller enters the doorway labeled "Guidance in the Building Up of the Personality," his multifaceted personality takes the form of pieces resembling chess pieces. Here, the process of re-integrating one's split personality, an integral part of the artist's "fine madness," is presented as a process of synthesizing the chess pieces into new, resolved wholes. This is what the building up of the personality means. For example, he is told: ". . . anyone whose soul has fallen to pieces . . . can rearrange these pieces of a previous self in what order he pleases, and so attain to an endless multiplicity of moves in the game of life."

Haller enters a door marked "Marvelous Training of the Steppenwolf" in which the man and the wolf are alternately dominating one another. Eventually, Haller has the taste of blood in his mouth. This is a particularly hellish sideshow and it concludes with Haller recalling the world war.

"All Girls Are Yours" presents a succession of flashing images of all the girls Haller has ever known in his life. He recalls Rosa Kreisler, in particular, in a setting much like Hesse's own Calw. Much of the sequence is similar in style and content to the pre-Romantic "Storm and Stress" literature.

The sideshow "How One Kills for Love" begins with a recollection of Hermine's having told Haller that he would "kill" her for love. Haller's "pieces" of his personality suddenly become a knife. In anguish, he runs about looking again for the chess master, but he suddenly sees a horrifying image of his tired, world-weary self in a full-length mirror. This uncreative, worldly self longs for death and, suddenly, strains from Mozart's opera *Don Giovanni* can be heard. It is the music that accompanies the approach of the white stone statue of the Commandant as this ghostly figure comes to deliver the unrepentant Don Giovanni to the demons of Hell for his murder. Ice-cold laughter rings out, "out of a world unknown to men, a world beyond all suffering, and born of the divine of divine humor." Then Mozart appears and Haller follows him into a dark compartment where the composer tells him that they are in the final act of *Don Giovanni*. Leporello, Don Giovanni's lackey and accomplice in murder, appears before us on his knees before the vengeful stone figure. Leporello is a kind of alter ego for Don Giovanni, who has allowed his worse self to control his actions.

Remarks are made about the decadence of composers after Mozart (Franz Schubert, Hugo Wolf, Frederick Chopin, and Ludwig von Beethoven) to the effect that there is something sinister and irrational lurking beneath the music of post-classicism, "beautiful as it may be . . . something rhapsodical about it, something of disintegration."

Then Mozart and Haller look to the images of more recent and even more decadent composers, such as Johannes Brahms and Richard Wagner. Mozart, who epitomized the lean clarity of classicism, regards the compositions of the late Romantics to bear excesses in orchestration and emotionality, "a fault of their time." Mozart impugns Haller and his vocation of writing by suggesting that Haller's work is merely plagiarized trivia. Haller, furious, grabs Mozart's queue which extends to such fantastic lengths that it resembles a comet with Haller still holding onto it as he flies into the furthest reaches of rarefied space. He lapses into a trance of icy gaiety in this realm of the beyond, after which he seems to lose consciousness altogether.

There is a break in the text at this point, and we now embark on Haller's gradual recovery to consciousness. Haller is fretful and suffering, his mind churning in the after-effects of intoxicants and strenuous mental exercise. One can observe, however, that certain bourgeois inhibitions have broken down for Haller, but that he still feels bound by time. There is still something awaiting Haller: he is to open a final door and, because he is nearly conscious, he will be vulnerable prey to his ego when his jealousy is aroused by the vision of Pablo with Hermine. Haller uses the knife on his other self, his "anima," which must be overcome, not destroyed. Pablo then leaves and smiles, knowing that Haller has fallen into the ego trap.

Suddenly, music can again be heard, and Mozart enters the compartment. He adroitly repairs a radio and tunes in a Munich broadcast of Handel's "Concerto Grosso in F Major," considered one of the finest of the Baroque master's compositions. The signal reception is quite distorted, which places a creative demand upon the listener to let his imagination compensate for the technical difficulties. Haller finds the broadcast to be sheer cacophony, not seeing that these emissions are merely a very imperfect copy of an indestructible original which is eternal. When Haller refers to the radio as a final weapon "in the war of extermination against art," Mozart merely laughs because he knows that the essence of the masterpiece transcends any radio transmission of it. Mozart directs Haller to the essence of Handel, imploring him to let the inspiration of Handel penetrate his "restless heart" and give it peace. The radio, he says, cannot destroy the original spirit of the music. Then Mozart makes his culminating remarks on the radio music of life, remarking that we must laugh rather than destroy, and that Haller attempted to destroy Hermine rather than laugh.

Memorable are Mozart's comments likening the mundane world and ego consciousness to a radio. The mundane life is a temporal projection of a higher reality, but it comes through like a poor signal in the Magic Theater. When Mozart remarks on Haller's desecration of the picture world of the Magic Theater, and says that killing Hermine was actually her own idea, Haller realizes that whatever was *her* idea was actually *his* as well. He recalls his former awareness of her role as his double, his shadow. Mozart laughs when Haller seems to realize the truth about himself. He also laughs at Haller's desire for self-punishment. In a way, Mozart's remark that humor is always "gallows humor" is almost a corollary to Miguel Unamuno's postulation of "the tragic sense of life" as a way to immunity from the events of this life which is, in turn, rooted to a longing for immortality. Interestingly, Hesse's work was so alluring to the Spanish-speaking world that it went into translation in the Romance languages (and even the Oriental languages) before it was translated into English.

At the end of this novel, a sign flashes before Haller's eyes which reads "Haller's Execution." His execution, however, is not what ordinary men would think of as a usual execution. Rather, it is an execution administered by the "madmen," the Immortals. Haller is sentenced to eternal life, and he is to be the object of the Immortals' endless laughter. Haller has misused the

Magic Theater, besmirching it with everyday reality; "he confounded our beautiful picture gallery with so-called reality."

Haller must listen to more of the "radio music of life" so that he can see the seemingly real in proper perspective as but a poor reflection of the ideal. Mozart here plays the role of the psychiatrist trying to orient the patient's mind in a forward, constructive direction, giving him an immediate goal ("listen to the cursed radio music of life . . . reverence the spirit behind it . . . laugh at its distortions"). Mozart suddenly mutates into his polar opposite, Pablo, who also comments on Haller's negative act of destruction in the picture world. The image of Hermine then takes the form of a tiny chess figure; and Pablo, the master of the game of personality building, puts it away in his pocket for next time. *Steppenwolf* has an unresolved but positive ending, for we are given to feel that there will be a "next time"—then Haller will have surely improved at this game. The game, with its little pieces, is a symbol for the path within, the glimpse into chaos which is the way to ultimate equilibrium.

From the standpoint of technique, this novel, which began in a basically realistic technique, has become radically surrealistic with its seemingly random succession of leitmotifs and allusions in the Magic Theater, which in turn presents an examination of the self from all sides and angles. This dissonant technique is consistent with the level-shifts and departures from ordinary reality in the story.

Above all, we must remember that what we read after the prologue in *Steppenwolf* is what Haller himself wrote and included and abandoned, hopefully along with his ego. As Haller's mental life increases in intensity toward the end of his stay at the landlady's house, his lattermost notes not only reflect this increased inner intensity, but they follow upon the heels of first-hand experience so closely that the experiences they relate have not as yet attained the distance in time perspective that would make them lend themselves to detached recounting. As a result, the cool realism of Haller's early memoirs gives way in the concluding ones to a surrealistic stream-of-consciousness.

CHARACTER ANALYSES

HARRY HALLER

Through Harry Haller's first-person narrative, we have some-what of an autobiographical projection of Hesse at the age of forty-eight. Haller feels that the different facets of his multiple man-wolf (will/intellect) personality will never complement one another, but will conflict with one another to the point of destruction, so he seriously entertains the idea of a shaving mishap on his fiftieth birthday to end it all. "Harry" is a nickname for Hermann, and it is no accident that Haller's initials are H. H. Likewise, it is not mere coincidence that Haller has sciatica, wears eyeglasses, has a library much like Hesse's grandfather's, and has anti-establishment ideas. Haller dislikes modern urban life as did Hesse, is politically committed against Germany's right-wing politics, and has premonitions of Germany's prepara-tions for the next war. We must note, also, that Haller's musical tastes lean toward those masters of supremely balanced form whose work predates the idea of *will* as a collective, positive Germanic force. Haller loves music which is uncontaminated by the manifestations of will in torrential, dissonant frenzy. Haller craves community with that corporate realm of Immortals who embody pure, self-disciplined intellect—Bach, Handel, and Mozart.

Haller, however, is not a musician; he is a writer—a creator of only subsidiary stature—and is aware that neither he nor any other men of his time can attain the stature of the Immortals. Writing fragments of less than great poetry and occasional es-says falls far short of the Kantian idealism of art for art's sake; thus Haller, with his middle-class background of which he is so wearily conscious, no doubt feels himself to be an ego-centered, will-imbued fraud like other twentieth-century men. Haller, however, is at least aware of his predicament—so much so that he alternates between Bürger and madman, becoming a vivid em-bodiment of the collective schizophrenia that he sees in

Germany. He is a victim of his own self-hate; his manuscript is his exorcism.

We learn, also, that a certain amount of Haller's psychological trouble can be rooted to his wife's insanity, which resulted in his leaving home as a kind of "non-person" — stripped of identity and manhood, according to bourgeois standards. Haller's agony lies in his divided self. He is part bourgeois in that he was brought up with middle-class values, is inclined at times toward orderliness and tidiness, and has tremendous feelings of guilt. He pays his taxes and owns corporate industrial securities, deriving his income from their dividends. But Haller is also part "wolf." His life style is essentially bohemian and he is resentful of the military-industrial complex which Germany has become. He is transfigured not by will but by intellect, by the ideal of eternal perfection which he believes exists in classical art, music particularly.

THE NEPHEW

The landlady's nephew has studied Greek and seems to have a consciousness of classical ideals which gives him the capacity to respond to the positive vein of Haller's manuscript. He is of Bürger stock, and his consuming hobby is tinkering with radios (the "wireless"). Even though his initial reaction to Haller is one of repugnance (a typical reaction of the supposedly healthy bourgeois toward those souls who appear to be sick), he grows progressively more interested in what seems to lie beneath the surface of Haller. After he salvages Haller's manuscript, he realizes that what lies beneath the surface of Haller, the individual, is what lies beneath the surface of twentieth-century man collectively. The nephew has the projection and insight to recognize that Haller's manuscript is a document of the abruptly changing times. As a bourgeois, the nephew also possesses that germ of will which gives him an interest in scientific advances. But he is also endowed with enough intellect to give him the capacity to respond positively to the seemingly irrational manuscript. The nephew and Haller complement one another because each is, in his own way, a divided personality, and each is strangely drawn toward the other's dominant world. Each becomes, in a sense, the other's "double."

THE AUNT

Some readers might be tempted to dismiss Haller's landlady as a typical "dear old lady" of the Bürger class. Indeed, she is a staunchly middle-class woman; she is a proud Bürger, dutifully keeping her house fastidiously tidy, as would any respectable lady of her station. There is, however, another side of the landlady's personality. She seems not to possess any of the negative attributes of the middle class. She is not meddlesome or gossipy. She seems to accept Haller's eccentricities and, rather than reacting with alarm, seems to like Haller. She is even mentioned in Haller's manuscript as inviting him to join her for tea, during which an interesting conversation ensues about the nephew's scientific bent and his love for the wireless.

THE PEDDLER

This street vendor hands Haller a little manual entitled "Treatise on the Steppenwolf." Harry reports seeing the peddler shortly after his vision of the sign "Magic Theater: Entrance Not For Everybody; For Madmen Only." The peddler also carries a sign about which Haller wants to inquire, but rather than answering Haller's inquiry about the advertisement, the peddler hands Haller the little handbook. Several days later, Haller sees the signbearer again and tries to inquire about the Magic Theater entertainments, but perhaps because Haller winks at him, he misunderstands and directs Haller to the notorious Black Eagle dance hall.

HERMINE

The name "Hermine" is a feminine form of "Hermann," and this peculiarly offbeat woman of the night is Haller's symbolic "double" or "anima" or "alter ego." Haller takes on a kind of apprenticeship under Hermine, who has rescued Haller in his night of despair, and they eventually engage in some unusual philosophical discussions. This philosophical and spiritual inclination in a woman of Hermine's calling seems to be a Dostoevskian influence, reminiscent particularly of Sonya in *Crime and Punishment.* Hermine tries to relieve Harry of his social awkwardness by teaching him how to dance and by exposing him to jazz. As the novel progresses, Hermine takes on different symbolic guises. At the Fancy Dress Ball, Hermine emerges as a hermaphrodite. Her ambiguity of gender gives her the appearance of a certain Hermann, a childhood friend of Harry's. Then she appears as a masked Pierrette. Finally, Hermine becomes part of the picture world reflected in Pablo's Magic Theater, and she symbolizes Haller's egotistical possessiveness of her. Haller attempts to destroy her because of a jealousy that proves that he has still not overcome polarity and egocentricity.

PABLO

Pablo is the dark, languid, saxophone-playing jazz musician who is the symbolic polar opposite to Mozart. He is thoroughly amoral and sensual. He is a creature of feeling and not of intellect. He resorts to drugs and is so non-verbal that, upon Haller's request to discuss music seriously with him, he withdraws, declaring that music is to be played—not discussed. It is Pablo's Magic Theater, however, that forms the nucleus of the Haller manuscript. It is Pablo's little mirror and his apparently faceted larger mirror that reflects with kaleidoscopic effect all the facets of the thousand-fold personality and all levels of consciousness.

REVIEW QUESTIONS

1. Discuss the parallels between Goethe's *Faust* and Hesse's *Steppenwolf.*

2. Relate Harry Haller's predicament in a bourgeois, urban milieu to his idealism.

3. Discuss the narrative points of view and the level shifts in *Steppenwolf.*

4. Discuss trends in post-classical and contemporary music as signs of decadence and decay as viewed by Haller's higher self.

5. Discuss the structural significance of the Treatise, the Goethe dream, and the Magic Theater.

6. Examine the nephew as an observer of Haller.

7. Discuss what the Mozart figure meant by referring to "radio music" in relation to the "life" of ordinary reality in the Magic Theater when he spoke of the "radio music of life" in distinguishing the real and the ideal.

8. In terms of the attainment of the deepest truths through what might appear to be insanity to ordinary men, discuss the meaning of the word "madmen."

9. Examine the polarities of Pablo/Mozart and of Hermine/Harry in terms of the many selves of Harry, and suggest how this is a microcosm of modern man.

10. Examine the role of Haller's manuscript as an enactment of Haller's fantasies, and suggest how the whole novel is, likewise, Hesse's enactment of Jungian visions and fantasies.

11. Compare and contrast, in terms of Oriental influence and in terms of the process of synthesis, *Siddhartha* and *Steppenwolf.*

12. How does Hermann Hesse's work fit into the perspective of twentieth-century surrealism?

Siddhartha Notes

INTRODUCTION

This novel is one of Hesse's finest and, certainly, is the finest product of Hesse's so-called psychoanalytic period. Begun in 1919, with its first section (through "Awakening") dedicated to the pacifist author Romain Rolland, the book's composition spanned nearly three years. The second section (through "By the River") was written during 1919-20, and the rest was completed eighteen months later. The entire work is loosely based on the life of Gotama Buddha. It also, however, bears a relationship to Hesse's own life for, like Siddhartha, Hesse decided to choose another career than that which his father suggested. Siddhartha left the strict bonds of his Brahmin father to seek his own salvation; Hesse left the strict bonds of his Pietist-Lutheran father to become a writer. Pietists, like Calvinists, believed that man is basically evil and thereby placed heavy emphasis on austere disciplinarianism. Likewise, Siddhartha's father was persistently performing ablutions at the river.

As for a similarity between the lives of Hesse's Siddhartha and the actual Buddha, we may observe that as a child, Siddhartha, like Buddha, was an outstanding pupil and athlete. He also left his wife and unborn son for the life of an ascetic, as did Buddha. Moreover, Buddha reportedly practiced yoga and meditated by the side of a river for six months. Also, as Siddhartha's most important decision comes to him under a mango tree, the most important decisions of the Buddha come to him in what are reported to be three visions under a Bo tree. In each case, it was beneath a tree by a river that the vision of all previous existences emerged in a revelation of the simultaneity of all things. Thus both men, by attaining Nirvana, were liberated from the vicious circle of metempsychosis and thereby attained salvation.

58

The Christian influence on *Siddhartha* may not be immediately obvious, but it is, nevertheless, unmistakable. To attain salvation, Siddhartha must once again regain his innocence, becoming once again as a little child before entering the Gates of Heaven. Herein lies the perfect resolution of the novel.

LIST OF CHARACTERS

Siddhartha

The protagonist of the novel, his life is vaguely based on that of Gotama Buddha (563?-483? B.C.), born Prince Siddhartha Gotama. Siddhartha is the personal name and means "he who is on the right road" or "he who has achieved his goal." Gotama is the clan name, and Buddha, which means "to know," is the title which his followers, who regarded him as almost a kind of god, gave to him.

Govinda

Siddhartha's dearest friend and confidant. He is Siddhartha's follower, his "shadow."

The Samanas

Three impoverished, emaciated ascetics who believe that temporal life is but an illusion; they practice extreme self-denial and meditation. Siddhartha and Govinda remain with the Samanas for three years.

Gotama Buddha

The "Illustrious," the "Enlightened," the "Sakyamuni" who achieved Nirvana, the supreme goal of Buddhism. "Sakyamuni" means the "Sage of the Sakyas" and is a title given to the Buddha by those outside of his clan. Nirvana is a form of salvation from the process of rebirth (which is the result of desire) by the extinguishing of desire. What the Buddhist seeks to avoid is separation from the whole of life, the unity of existence. The life-death-rebirth cycle, rooted in the concept of the transmigration of souls, separates man from the whole and is thereby associated with evil. The Buddhist endeavors to extinguish desire and thereby suspend this cycle. The process of passing from one form of existence to another is suppressed by high aspiration, purity of life, and the elimination of the ego. The resulting suspension of the rebirth cycle is accompanied by a state in which man ceases to exist and, instead of becoming, he attains Being. Thought is the highest faculty of man and meditation holds a prominent place in the final steps of his deliverance. Buddha is nearly always depicted as sitting with his legs crossed and his feet facing upwards, the posture of meditation he had assumed under the Bo tree when he achieved enlightenment. The Buddha, although not a god, embodies the ideal of what any man may become; Buddhism seeks to vitalize this ideal in the minds of believers.

Kamala

The courtesan from the city who claims that she is capable of dispensing and teaching love as an art, but who appears later among the followers of Buddha. In the city, Kamala is the embodiment of sensual desire, the polar opposite of Nirvana. She brings Siddhartha his son eleven years later; later still, she dies of snakebite.

Kamaswami

The rich merchant for whom Siddhartha worked in the city. His name means "master of the material world."

Vasudeva

The ferryman who takes Siddhartha across the river and with whom Siddhartha is later to live and work. Vasudeva is serene and enlightened and tells Siddhartha what the river can teach. Siddhartha eventually succeeds Vasudeva as the ferryman. Vasudeva is another name for Krishna, who is the teacher of Arjuna (the principal hero of the *Bhagavad-Gita*) and a human incarnation of Vishnu, a Hindu deity.

CRITICAL COMMENTARIES

THE BRAHMIN'S SON

The novel begins with a brief retrospective glance at Siddhartha's Brahmin (priestly Hindu caste) family background, his upbringing, and the innocence and tranquility of his childhood. We are promptly aligned with Siddhartha at the threshold of young manhood and simultaneously observe the orthodox Brahmin father of Siddhartha who, with his son, performs the rite of ablution at the river. Later, as we meet Govinda, Siddhartha's boyhood friend and close comrade, we feel them to be so close intellectually and fraternally that they are almost one.

In spite of the admiration and adoration which Siddhartha receives from his family and friends, his soul is perpetually restless and fraught with disquieting dreams. Unable to find inner peace, Siddhartha initiates his search for Atman. He knows that Atman, the individual spirit or Self, is within him and is inclined toward Brahman (the supreme universal Soul), and he strives to find his own way to experience Atman. Siddhartha is troubled by the fact that nobody—not the wisest teachers, or his father, or the holy songs—can lead him to the discovery of Self. Teachers and scripture have yielded only second-hand learning, not the first-hand experience from which knowledge emanates. Siddhartha suggests that his father, like himself, must not be actually experiencing Atman, for he continually performs ablutions to absolve himself of spiritual impurity and guilt. (The individual soul will not merge with the all-perfect Being unless the individual soul is cleansed of guilt.)

Up to this point, the passage of time has been vague and barely perceptible, but we are suddenly made conscious of a specific evening. It is important to note that this time pattern continues throughout *Siddhartha:* years pass imperceptibly; then, a day and a half or two days will suddenly emerge as strikingly distinct. Now, the Samanas are briefly described, and on this specific evening, Siddhartha breaks the news to Govinda that he has decided to free himself from his predetermined Hindu caste and plans to leave his father to join the Samanas. After standing on his feet all night in defiant endurance and upon receiving reluctant consent from his father, Siddhartha leaves home at daybreak. The father alludes to his own spiritual disquietude as Siddhartha departs, and he asks his son to teach bliss to him should he find it in the forest among the Samanas. Govinda's shadow then appears and he joins Siddhartha.

We have now been introduced to two important motifs — the river and the shadow. The river is introduced as a cleansing agent, and Govinda, who will part ways with Siddhartha and again rejoin him, is Siddhartha's shadow. Among the important themes of the book is the father-son theme, which will be re-established at the end of the novel with Siddhartha's defiant, prodigal son leaving him. Also introduced in this section is Hesse's unique handling of time through compressing longer time periods and unexpectedly expanding shorter time periods. The syllable "OM," the sacred syllable of the Hindu yoga breathing exercise, is introduced and we become aware that concentration on the word — and abstraction from all mundane things — will enhance unity with Brahman and will suspend the concept of time.

Another of the important considerations in this section is this: for Siddhartha, Atman is all-perfect. The god Prajapati is not nearly so important to Siddhartha because Prajapati was created. Siddhartha concedes more attributes of deity to Atman, for a created god, like anything else created, emanates from something else and is thereby not a first cause. But Siddhartha is not able to evoke Atman at will. Atman is discovered only after the ego is negated and the conscious and the unconscious are resolved through synthesis. References to the Hindu scriptures, the *Vedas* (specifically the *Rig Veda*) and the *Chandogya-Up-anishads*, are made but they do not satisfy Siddhartha because they do not show him the way, even though they contain learned material. In short, it is becoming evident already that Siddhartha is a rebel; he must think for himself. He is not a ready-made disciple.

WITH THE SAMANAS

It is in this sequence that Siddhartha and Govinda attempt to gain salvation through asceticism. Using as a premise the ascetic idea that the sensual world is transitory and illusory, Siddhartha attempts to void his self and thus void with it all the torments of the senses. He resolves that if he can let the self die, then something deeper than the self will surface — that is, Being. Siddhartha, however, finds the process of trying to void the self a vicious circle because even though the ascetic meditation of which the aim is emptying the self involves the assuming of different forms, it inevitably leads him back to self again. All the paths leading away from self eventually lead back to it and are particularly tormenting because, like the life cycle, they are imbued with a sense of time. Thus Siddhartha regards this as just another form of escapism, in this case through self-denial, just as drinking is escapism through self-indulgence. Even though Govinda states that he is still learning, Siddhartha asserts that he himself is far from knowledge and wisdom.

After the imperceptible passage of three years with the Samanas, Siddhartha resolves to leave them. Not only does Siddhartha again object to discipleship and assert the impossibility of learning things second-hand, he asserts that learning impedes knowledge. Govinda is, of course, troubled by Siddhartha's lecture. At this point, we learn of the arrival of Gotama Buddha, who has conquered sorrow and brought the cycle of rebirth to a standstill. He has attained Nirvana; he remembers former lives and will never return to the cycle. Govinda enjoins Siddhartha to go and hear the teachings of Buddha. Siddhartha is amazed that Govinda (heretofore always Siddhartha's shadow) is initiating a course of action, and since Siddhartha desires to go, they both decide to leave the Samanas. Here we have another time expansion, a kind of enlargement of a particular day when a specific allusion is made to "the same day," and Siddhartha draws the angry Samana teacher into the same hypnotic spell that the teacher himself had taught.

Important in this section is the fact that living among the ascetics dissatisfies Siddhartha for the same reason that Brahminism never really satisfied his father. As the rules and rituals of the Brahmin priests did not provide knowledge through experience, likewise the Samana rules and ascetic observances do not either. Instead, they are merely a kind of escapism. Supremely important is the fact of Gotama Buddha's having attained Nirvana, transcending and suspending the transmigratory life cycle and the agony of time.

GOTAMA

In this sequence, Siddhartha goes with Govinda to hear the teachings of Buddha, and Govinda remains with Buddha to become his disciple. Siddhartha, however, feels that everyone must find his own way to salvation and, hence, does not remain. The "Gotama" sequence begins with Buddha's taking alms in the town of Savathi and his abiding in the Jetavana grove.

Reference is made to a specific night when a lady tells Siddhartha and Govinda that they may sleep among the pilgrims. By daybreak, the town is swarming with the followers of Gotama Buddha, and Siddhartha and Govinda see him for the first time. Despite his commonplace appearance and traditional yellow monk's garb, he stands out because he radiates inner peace. It is during this day that we learn of Siddhartha's affinity to Buddha and his complete love for him for possessing truth, knowledge, and peace. However, we learn that despite his attraction toward Buddha, Siddhartha is adamant in his disinterest in teachings.

That evening, Buddha preaches before the crowd that there is salvation from pain and suffering for those who follow the prescribed course of Buddhism—that is, the Four Noble Truths —of which the fourth involves the taking of the Eightfold Path. Govinda volunteers to join the Buddhist pilgrims and hopes that Siddhartha will also join. Siddhartha, however, declines, and the impending separation of the two boyhood friends brings tears to their eyes. After their fraternal embrace and Govinda's taking the monk's habit, Siddhartha wanders through the grove and meets Gotama. They engage in a deep conversation in which Siddhartha extols Gotama's doctrine of understanding the world as a complete, unbroken, eternal chain, linked together by cause and effect. It is in this conversation that Siddhartha points out that the doctrine of salvation is neither shown nor proven. Gotama concedes the flaw in logic but asserts that his message is not for the intellectually curious, but that he seeks only to teach salvation. Siddhartha again voices the central idea of the novel: he reminds the Buddha that the process of enlightenment which he underwent is unteachable, that there is no way of communicating first-hand experience to disciples. One can find the secret of self-realization only by going one's own way. Siddhartha, speaking only for himself and not for the other pilgrims, tells of his resolve to leave all doctrines and all teachers behind and to reach his goal alone. As they part, the smile of the Buddha remains in Siddhartha's mind, and he associates it with a man who has conquered his self. And even though Siddhartha feels that he has lost his friend Govinda to Buddha, he feels that he has gained something from Buddha—the inspiration of direct, firsthand contact with the Illustrious One, which further strengthens his resolve to conquer self. Yet Siddhartha again rejects formal doctrine for the same reason as before: enlightenment defies structured doctrine and transcends the teaching process.

The formal doctrine of Buddhist salvation is briefly as follows: it includes a system of which the keys are alluded to in the text—that is, the Four Noble Truths and the Eightfold Path. The Four Noble Truths include (1) the existence of pain, (2) pain's cause being desire or attachment, (3) the possibility of enduring pain by suppressing desire, and (4) the Eightfold Path to salvation. This path involves right faith, right life, right language, right purpose, right practice, right effort, right thinking, and right meditation. The link between this system and salvation lies in a "chain of causation," which is based on the cause-effect relationship between desire and pain. The root cause of pain is birth (which arises from desire), for the consequence of birth is exposure to time, illness, and death. Birth is but one point in the transmigration of souls inherent in the life cycle.

Of the important motifs of the novel, the one which is introduced in the "Gotama" sequence is that of the smile. It is evoked from self-realization and will appear again in the final section of the novel.

AWAKENING

This brief sequence portends a basic turning point in the novel and signals the end of Part I. The mood of this sequence is one of great loneliness, for Siddhartha is beyond the point of being able to return home again, and now he has parted ways with Govinda. He reflects that he has left his former life behind him and has now matured from youth to manhood. He again contemplates the limitations of teachers and reflects that among the things that they cannot teach is the matter of the self. The tone approaches despair as Siddhartha seeks to rid himself of self, or at least to try to flee from self. He sees that there is nothing about which he knows less than his self. He reflects that his lack of knowledge of his self grew out of fear and the desire to flee, and that in his search for Atman he became lost. He feels an awakening and asserts that he will no longer try to escape from Siddhartha. He believes now that he can slough off his search for Atman, his asceticism, and the scriptures. He resolves to learn the secret of Siddhartha from himself.

At this point, all the world around Siddhartha exudes the colorations of sensual beauty, and he is at the brink of the theory that reality is in the world itself, the sensual world. He feels that he has suddenly awakened. Then an icy chill comes over him as he realizes that he is completely alone. Having shed the old skin of meditation, he realizes now that he is not the Brahmin's son any more. Realizing that he belongs to no family or peer group whatever, he falls into a spasm of despair, while at the same time he feels more firmly himself than ever. As Siddhartha experiences the pangs of this awakening, he resolves to never again "walk backwards."

This "Awakening" sequence terminates Part I and prefigures Siddhartha's crossing the river to enter into the sensual world of the city with the beautiful courtesan Kamala. The metaphorically rich imagery of a snake molting its old skin anticipates a later appearance of this popular Indian motif.

KAMALA

Unlike Part I, the second part of this novel was written with extreme difficulty. Part I, Hesse said, flowed in a potent burst of creative energy, but this creative energy seemed suddenly to run dry; Hesse didn't know how to continue his story or how to end it, so he put the manuscript away for about eighteen months. One would never guess, however, that Hesse had problems with this section. It begins with a superb lyric passage extolling the wonders of the tangible world. Its descriptions of nature have a lulling, trancelike quality, swirling with color and suggestion. The prose is almost biblical, awesome and spellbinding. And beneath the prose, we discern the familiar Hesse theme of *Natur/Geist*—the temporal realm and the spiritual realm residing on opposite sides of reality—the temporal world on this side of reality and the permanent world on the other side. Now we will learn about the impact of Siddhartha's three years with the Samanas. Despite the allurements of the sensual world of *Natur*, Samana life has so conditioned Siddhartha that he will be capable of realizing the nature/spirit dichotomy. Siddhartha's inner voice, though neglected, is never quite extinguished.

The "Kamala" sequence, like previous sequences, seems to hover for some time in expository prose, undelineated in definite time, and then suddenly Hesse zooms in for a close-up of a particular day and a half, beginning with a night and continuing through the next day. The events of this particular night and the following day are extremely important in the development of the rest of the novel because they are heavy with symbols and motifs that are used in later sections of the novel. For example, Siddhartha sleeps in a ferryman's hut; the ferryman will be the key figure in Siddhartha's self-resolution and synthesis. Also, the dream which Siddhartha has in the hut is not only full of Jungian symbolism, but it is also the vehicle by which the worlds of sense and spirit are united. Govinda, Siddhartha's shadow (the Jungian other self), appears in that dream as not only Siddhartha's shadow, but also as a hermaphrodite — that is, a symbol of the "anima" (the weak, sensually oriented, female component of the total personality). There is also the symbolism of the beginning of life, of oneness, in the maternal images associated with the female element in the dream. The sense of the flow of life and of oneness can also be associated symbolically with the ferryman's hut, perhaps itself a womb symbol because it will be the ferryman who will be instrumental in Siddhartha's union with the river, a symbol of beginning and of life.

The day after Siddhartha has his dream is significant because it is during this time that Siddhartha meets the ferryman and hears his remarks about one's being able to "learn" from the river. The river, of course, is an archetypal symbol, and here it is the symbolic boundary between the two worlds of sense and spirit. Siddhartha regards his meeting the ferryman as a mere accident, but the ferryman's comments about Siddhartha's destiny to return eventually are structurally and philosophically important. One of the secrets of the river that the ferryman has learned, and one which Siddhartha will finally learn, is that all things eventually return. Like primal waters, everything is imbued with the quality of recurrence. There is no death. There is no time. The river is timeless, ever-changing and yet changeless. Siddhartha, however, is too involved in pursuing the education of his senses to fathom the significance of his conversation with the ferryman and so he dismisses him as, for the present, merely a likeable, Govinda-like person.

After having passed the river and the ferryman, Siddhartha finally has his first glimpse of Kamala in the late afternoon. He resolves to shed his beggar's appearance, fearing that Kamala would scorn him. The night passes and on the following day, Siddhartha manipulates his meeting with Kamala, who recalls Siddhartha's deferential bow of the previous afternoon. Siddhartha beseeches Kamala to be his teacher, and we see Kamala's utterly materialistic values in her demand that Siddhartha have fine clothes and shoes. When the question arises as to what Siddhartha can do to earn a living, he can only remember the virtues of thinking, waiting, and fasting which he learned as a Samana. Shortly, however, it is discovered that he can read and write, whereupon he is considered valuable enough to become the partner of the rich merchant Kamaswami. It is even suggested in Kamala's remarks that Siddhartha might be qualified to succeed Kamaswami, for a remark is made about the rich merchant's advanced age. The observant reader, however, can sense that he is not the man whose place Siddhartha will take. In this city, Siddhartha will no more learn love from Kamala's teaching than would he have learned truth from the Hindus' or Buddhists' or Samanas' teachings. But Siddhartha will never quite lose those arts which he learned as a Samana. It will be by way of the conditioning inherent in thinking, waiting, and fasting that he will attain the capacity to attain his goal. Siddhartha, of course, means "he who attains his goal."

AMONGST THE PEOPLE

This second sequence of Part II develops Siddhartha's acquaintance with Kamala and introduces Siddhartha to Kamaswami. Significant is the meaning inherent in names, beginning with "Kama"; Kama is the Hindu god of lustful love and desire. The word "swami" designates Kamaswami as a master—in this case, the master of the hedonistic, worldly realm.

We can begin to see the conditioning of the Samanas surfacing when Siddhartha takes an indifferent attitude toward business, possessions, and worldly people. Siddhartha can sense that he is different from these worldly "child-people," but he finds this distinction between himself and them problematical. Siddhartha's spiritual background has only partially enlightened him for he has not yet found peace, and he comes to envy these ordinary, unintellectual people. Kamala, nevertheless, is attracted to Siddhartha because of his detachment, this refuge which she feels that only the two of them have. Likewise,

Kamala's detachment will also become problematical for it will be discovered that love cannot be dispensed as an art. The most significant event of this section is Siddhartha's mentioning Gotama Buddha to Kamala for the first time. To Siddhartha, Buddha exemplifies the kind of man who possesses a special guide and wisdom within himself. This conversation is of particular significance because it prefigures Kamala's future destiny. The eventual coming of Kamala's future son is also signaled at this point. The sequence ends with a verbal exchange on the subject of love, significant because an inability to love will be the source of both Kamala's and Siddhartha's despair.

SANSARA

We plumb the depths of the world of illusion in the sequence entitled "Sansara." Sansara, the polar opposite of Nirvana, is identified in the Buddhist system with illusion, spiritual death, and ultimate despair. Many years pass during this sequence that takes place in the city, and the fine poetic image of the potter's wheel symbolizes Siddhartha's spiritual awareness grinding to a halt. Siddhartha has abandoned his soul for a life that will become a barren, sterile waste for him, and because Siddhartha is an intellectual, ennui and soul sickness set in. Siddhartha becomes obsessively acquisitive and yet, at heart, he is contemptuous of wealth; again, then, he is part of a vicious circle. In this temporal, hedonistic world of the city, time is the devourer of all things. Herein lies the root of Siddhartha's suffering; all that is imbued with the element of time is doomed to death.

Also in the "Sansara" sequence, we again experience one of Hesse's close-ups — in this instance, Siddhartha is reminded of a peculiar dream on a certain evening. Siddhartha, so thoroughly conditioned by his life with the Samanas, is utterly unfulfilled by the superficiality of life with the child-people. He reflects on the elements of time and aging, retires after midnight, and puts in a night of complete personal misery. It is only at dawn that he sleeps at all, at which time he has the dream of which he seems to have been reminded the evening before. It is a highly symbolic dream in which a primal element of nature is the key symbol. He dreams of Kamala's little pet bird, symbolic of Siddhartha's spiritual self which he now believes to be dead. He reflects upon the desert of his soul and resolves that because his life among the child-people is a slow, corrosive death, he must leave the city that night. The sterile life of the city has become a prison for his soul as the cage is a prison for the little songbird.

BY THE RIVER

As we embark upon this sequence, we must realize that Siddhartha is now in his forties and that he has spent a little over twenty years in the city. Time rushes by in this novel very much like a current beneath the time close-ups. Plot progression seemingly takes place only when we zoom in on isolated days and nights, yet the story unfolds continually and unrelentingly. The sense of undercurrent becomes even more awesome in the sequences involving Siddhartha at the river with Vasudeva. We learn what Siddhartha is to learn: the river subsumes all time, all creation, all destruction. It is timeless and transcendent. Here, Vasudeva's prophecy of roughly twenty years earlier is fulfilled: everything does indeed return, even Siddhartha. Vasudeva will conquer his antithesis (Kamaswami) and we are gradually prepared for Siddhartha's succeeding Vasudeva. Upon Siddhartha's initial return to the river, prior to the actual encounter with Vasudeva, he begins his self-restoration. He hears the Brahmins' sacred syllable for the unity of all being—OM—as it wells up from his soul and forms a bond with the water. The transcendent OM of the river lulls Siddhartha into a trancelike sleep from which he later awakens, refreshed and face-to-face with Govinda. Siddhartha and the Buddhist monk Govinda have a talk, from which a basic revelation emerges: the cause of Siddhartha's soul sickness is an inability to love. The syllable OM had awakened this revelation within Siddhartha's soul and seeing Govinda has brought it to the surface. Siddhartha then regains his lost innocence and smiles.

With Siddhartha's spiritual restoration, already time begins to dissolve, to fall away. Large parts of this sequence are devoted

to solitary reflection in which Siddhartha realizes that it is not
the bird of his innermost soul that has died, but his conscious,
grasping egotistical self. The process of synthesis is an agonizing
process, an ordeal of sansara and self-realization, of individuation, from which resolution and equilibrium are to come forth.
As Siddhartha reflects on salvation, he is also aware that his inner voice is still there. He is a newly awakened, innocent and
childlike Siddhartha, endowed now with the capacity to love the
flowing waters of the river. The river is the agent through which
Siddhartha will plumb the depths of his consciousness — a kind
of psychoanalysis, as it were.

THE FERRYMAN

Vasudeva, the quiet ferryman whose name is derived from
one of the names of Krishna, and which basically means "he in
whom all things abide and who abides in all," is an unforgettable
character. In Siddhartha's decision to stay by the river, he recalls
the ferryman and resolves that his new life will begin again with
the ferryman. Siddhartha's inner synthesis will be effected
through a resolution of permanence and transience — and it is
Vasudeva, as well as Siddhartha's own inner voice, which affirms
that the river will prove to be the agent of Siddhartha's fulfillment. As Siddhartha requests that Vasudeva take him across,
Siddhartha is completely absorbed by the tranquil human presence of the ferryman, as earlier he had been by that of Gotama
Buddha.

The key to learning from the river, according to Vasudeva,
is *listening*. We will discover, however, that before Vasudeva's
knowledge can be of any significance to Siddhartha, it must be
tempered with love. What Siddhartha learns from Vasudeva is
an affirmation of life and a sense of harmony with nature.

After Vasudeva tells Siddhartha that the river has spoken to
him, he tells Siddhartha that he will learn two things from the
river. Already he has learned one of these: to strive downwards
like a stone. Vasudeva cannot tell Siddhartha what the other

thing to be learned will be, for it is a form of intuitive experience which defies verbalization. Vasudeva then tells Siddhartha about the job of ferryman, his task being to take people across the river and to give them directions once they get across. Symbolically, his task is to show men the way to salvation. He can only show the way, however. Men must attain salvation themselves. The conversation continues through the evening and into the night and, at its end, the narrative lapses into indefinite time.

One of the outstanding conversations of the entire novel occurs when Siddhartha asks Vasudeva about time. The ferryman tells him of the transcendent timelessness of the river, which brings Siddhartha to the realization that life is also a river and that past, present, and future are all one. Childhood, adulthood, and old age are separated only by shadows, not by reality. This, basically, is Siddhartha's Nirvana. This mystical union with simultaneity, with Brahma, forms the nucleus of the book. The conversation then culminates with Siddhartha's equating time with suffering, another basic idea of the book. We are reminded that the river embodies all creation, all layers of consciousness: it is the collective unconscious of man's ancestral soul in its ten thousand voices, and the eternal OM brings them to the surface of our consciousness simultaneously. The two ferrymen, Vasudeva and Siddhartha, become as brothers, united by the sacred river.

Years pass and we come to learn that Gotama Buddha is on the threshold of eternal salvation and his Buddhist followers are gathering to their teacher for the last time. Siddhartha recalls the living presence of the Buddha which has awed him so much, and he feels a strong bond with him.

The montage narrative again zooms into a definite time sequence as we observe the day when Kamala and her eleven-year-old son come to see Buddha. The observant reader somehow knows now that Kamala has been attracted to the life of the Buddhist monks, for she made a direct inquiry about Gotama when Siddhartha was taking leave of the city. The father-son motif is soon to be re-established, and we are to realize that the boy is one of the child-people. We are, however, given little hints that this boy will eventually seek his own goals despite his current recalcitrance. The most substantial hint lies in the fact that the boy is called "little Siddhartha."

After the events of the day, Siddhartha has another of his visions of the mystical transcendence of the river and of its transcendence of time, experiencing again the simultaneity and unity of all life. The next morning, as preparations are made for Kamala's pyre, Siddhartha's hopes are directed toward his son.

THE SON

As this sequence begins, the action occurs on no particular day or any particular time of day; we are simply given a report of the father-son relationship. The sadness of the events which follow are sublimely tempered by the wisdom and kindness of the old Vasudeva. Despite Siddhartha's efforts to win the love and respect of his son, the son is more drawn to the enticements of the city, the milieu of his mother, than to the spiritual leanings of his stranger-father. Vasudeva reminds Siddhartha that, like his father, the boy will have to rebel, that he too must run away and learn things for himself.

Earlier the ferryman told Siddhartha that he would soon be learning something that he could not verbalize, and Siddhartha now realizes what it is as he looks into his son's face. The child's face evokes the memory of Kamala when she and Siddhartha told each other that they were incapable of love, and that it was this that separated them from ordinary people. Because of the anguish of this memory, Siddhartha realizes that he not only loves the river, but that—like ordinary men—he loves another person— the essence of Kamala in little Siddhartha.

The time comes when Siddhartha must accept little Siddhartha's departure. Little Siddhartha runs away bitterly from his father, returns late in the evening, and departs across the symbolic river with Siddhartha and Vasudeva following—not, as

Vasudeva warns, to catch him, but to observe him and to retrieve the boat. Vasudeva's laughter concerning the boy's departure is not the cruel laugh of ridicule, but a sublime laugh embodying Vasudeva's knowledge of the boy's way—that is, his destiny, meaning that all things return. Siddhartha wants to spare his son from the grueling ordeal of sansara, but Vasudeva knows that this is impossible. Siddhartha has a sudden visionary glimpse of the city and sees that Kamala converted her pleasure garden into a refuge for Buddhist monks. His mind returns to the early days when he first saw the rich Kamala from outside, when he was a poor Samana; recalling the processes of life and death, he remembers the syllable OM, symbolized by the caged songbird. The sense of loss because of his son's abrupt departure lingers in Siddhartha like a deep wound. For the first time, Siddhartha has direct, firsthand experience with the pain of love.

OM

This sequence begins with the wound motif and traces Siddhartha's recovery from the sickness he felt because of his son. Its primary material concerns the sense of simultaneity and unity within Siddhartha, expressed by the river's utterance of OM. It ends with Siddhartha's succeeding Vasudeva as the ferryman of the river.

Still suffering from his wound, Siddhartha hears the sublime laugh of the river. He sees his face reflected in the river and he recognizes his father in it, thereby effecting a unity with his father, who also experienced Siddhartha's "wound." Siddhartha's solitary meditation beside the river is broken by a compelling desire to go to Vasudeva, to confess his wound and its source to Vasudeva, and to disclose his guilt feelings. Vasudeva, the sublime listener whose very presence is transcendent, becomes like the river itself; Siddhartha's baring his soul to him has the effect of bathing his wound in the river. Vasudeva tells Siddhartha that, even though he has heard the ten thousand voices of the river and its laugh, he will hear yet something more from it. Siddhartha then sees many pictures and hears a voice of sorrow in the river. As he watches and listens, the text moves into a beautiful lyric passage embodying the liquid, eternal feel of the river itself. Siddhartha now feels that he has completely mastered the art of listening as he listens further and hears the voices of the river coalesce into perfection: OM. Following this experience, he sees Vasudeva's smile and realizes that his wound has healed.

GOVINDA

As this sequence begins, Govinda has arrived to cross the river, meeting Siddhartha, who is now an old man. Siddhartha's eyes smile as did Vasudeva's many years earlier. A superlative dialogue between them follows in which Siddhartha declares that in order to find one's goal, one must be free. The goal, Nirvana, is so elusive as to defy formulation, and too much seeking on the *conscious* level can make fulfillment impossible. Govinda knows that Siddhartha has found his own way and realizes that he did it without the formal system of Buddhist doctrine. As the Buddha tried long ago, Siddhartha now tries to express how he found his way, but verbalization cannot create or invoke the intuitive, transcendent experience for Govinda. As Siddhartha invites Govinda to stay with him in his hut for the night, we come to another close-up time sequence.

On the following morning, after Govinda asks Siddhartha about any doctrine which he might have, Siddhartha tries to explain how he attained inner peace from Vasudeva and the river rather than from teachers. He then draws the distinction between knowledge and wisdom, remarking that wisdom cannot be imparted from one man to another. Knowledge may be acquired from teachers, but wisdom must come from direct experience. Siddhartha then offers his thoughts on truth, suggesting that if an attempt is made at putting truth into words, something is always inherently missing. Verbalization eliminates that other side of a truth which defies verbalization. All that is thought and expressed verbally is, in fact, only a half-truth. Also, in every truth which is complete, not only does the truth which appears exist, but its antithesis also inherently exists.

This section reveals that not only Samana life left its mark on Siddhartha, but that his brief contact with the Buddha left its mark also. Buddhist doctrine is predicated on the antithetical elements of Nirvana and sansara; all truth possesses these two opposites—the truth side and the illusion side, all things being imbued with salvation and suffering. The speech concludes in a final excursis on time: if time is not real, then the line between this world and eternity is also not real. Siddhartha uses the example of a stone and suggests that because it is but one part of the whole cycle of life and thereby has transmigratory potential, it is consequently not just a stone but at once God and Buddha. We come back to the idea that all things return—that the stone has been all else and will again become all else.

Words, however, are not endowed with transmigratory potential. Thoughts, which are also mere verbalizations, are not so endowed either. After once again extolling Vasudeva, Siddhartha concludes his discourse by declaring that love is the most important thing in the world. We can sense that he feels that Gotama Buddha also embraced love—despite his verbalizations to the contrary, and Siddhartha projects this contradiction as just cause for being distrustful of words. He extols Gotama, but Govinda admits that he still has not found peace. Govinda has a sudden, transcendent, verbally inexpressible experience in the awesome presence of Siddhartha, much like that which Siddhartha had in the presence of Vasudeva years earlier.

When Siddhartha summons Govinda to kiss him on the forehead, Govinda feels as if he is touching eternity, a kind of mystical transference from Siddhartha, and he sees in Siddhartha's beatific smile a continuous stream of thousands of faces much like those Siddhartha saw many years earlier in the river. Like Siddhartha, Govinda attains Nirvana, reaching the depths of the ancestral soul of man, the Jungian collective unconscious.

CHARACTER ANALYSES

SIDDHARTHA

The preeminent factor in a study of Hesse's Hindu protagonist is his growth from the impatience and impetuosity of youth and young adulthood to the fulfilled wisdom of age. Despite the fact that Siddhartha leaves his father, the influence of his Brahmin upbringing stays with him, for the goal of his life is the attainment of Nirvana. It is merely the means to the end with which he disagrees with his father and also with the Samanas, Gotama Buddha, and the Buddha-follower Govinda. The growth pattern of Siddhartha's entire life consists of several phases of conditioning which are necessary to attain a perfect unity with the Absolute. Siddhartha must experience Brahman spontaneously and without artificial preparation in order to transcend time and gain Nirvana. In all stages of his life, Siddhartha must, as his name suggests, "seek his own goal" in an untutored, unassisted first-hand quest. His traversing the river into the city is, likewise, an integral phase of the quest. The transparency of this illusory world only becomes apparent to Siddhartha after he has had the chance to experience this time-bound world directly. The despair which follows prepares us for the final realization of a middle-aged Siddhartha: pursuing the way of the sense deity, Kama, will lead to nothingness. Vasudeva completes Siddhartha's entry into his final stage of self-realization by *not* attempting to teach or indoctrinate, but by showing Siddhartha that the inexplicable ways of the river promise revelation.

KAMALA

We first encounter this attractive courtesan upon Siddhartha's arrival in the city of child-people; she is the "queen" of the Hindu art of love. Then, as life in the city becomes transparently illusory for her, as it did for Siddhartha, she seems to realize that love cannot be dispensed secondhand, as an art form.

There is a subtle pause in the role of Kamala in the plot after we follow Siddhartha out of the city, but it is strongly hinted that she will reappear later as a changed person. She emerges finally as a Buddhist and we learn that she transcended the "art" of love by directly experiencing it with Siddhartha. Her being carried off from this world in Vasudeva's hunt bears symbolic significance to her transformation.

GOVINDA

The primary significance of Govinda in the novel as a secondary character is his attaining Nirvana, a growth similar to Siddhartha's, but delayed somewhat because of his function as Siddhartha's "shadow." Govinda is slower to realize that Nirvana does not come after years of study and learning; in contrast, Siddhartha seems already to know this when Govinda joins Gotama Buddha. Their parting at that strategic point serves to reinforce the importance of direct, firsthand experience when they reunite at the river. Govinda has come the way of Siddhartha, but on his own — not as a disciple or as a follower of Siddhartha. Govinda's attaining the transcendent beatific smile and union with the river of life is, therefore, his own. Most important, he has accomplished this in the only way one can — independently.

REVIEW QUESTIONS

1. How does Siddhartha's life with the Samanas condition him for his process of self-recognition?

2. What is the function of the river and of Vasudeva in this novel?

3. Discuss the father-son theme.

4. Examine the process of synthesis as it relates to Hesse's contact with Jungianism and relate its thematic influence in a selected novel.

5. Examine Hesse's treatment of time lapses in this novel, focusing on the close-up technique for extending short spans of time, and the "telephoto" effect for foreshortening long spans of time.

6. Siddhartha and Buddha both eventually attain Nirvana. However, the way that each achieves it is different. Explain the difference, relating this to the reason for Siddhartha's not following the Buddha.

7. What is the function of Kamala in the novel?

Selected Bibliography

BAUMER, FRANZ. *Hermann Hesse*. New York: Frederick Ungar Publishing Company, 1969. This work originally appeared in Berlin in 1959, remaining untranslated into English for ten years. It is a delightfully readable little book and presents a vivid study of the contemplative and solitary Hermann and Ninon Hesse of the Ticine years.

BOULBY, MARK. *Hermann Hesse: His Mind and Art*. Ithaca, New York: Cornell University Press, 1968. This is a very detailed study of the imagery, language, and intricate motif patterns in Hesse's novels and poems. It is a study of form; hence, its focus and emphasis goes beyond facts and biography.

FIELD, GEORGE WALLIS. *Hermann Hesse*. New York: Twayne Publishers, Inc., 1970. This book is a comprehensive and detailed study of the novels of Hesse, augmented by biographical and factual information.

FREEDMAN, RALPH. *The Lyrical Novel*. Princeton: Princeton University Press, 1962. Now in a paperback edition, this book centers its focus on novelists whose works deal with autobiographical revelation and poetic depths rather than conventional plot. Various sections are devoted to, besides Hesse, Andre Gide and Virginia Woolf.

MILECK, JOSEPH. *Hermann Hesse and His Critics*. New York: AMS Press, Inc., 1966. This is one of the finest academic studies of Hesse in English, containing a detailed and authoritative biographical section, a bibliography of works on Hesse in many languages, and commentaries on the major books, monographs, and articles. This book may be difficult for some undergraduates because some of its quotations and references remain in the original German.

ROSE, ERNST. *Faith from the Abyss: Hermann Hesse's Way from Romanticism to Modernity.* New York: New York University Press, 1965. This highly readable volume is now in paperback, and it presents poignant and useful biographical information relating it to the changes in the author's many works. It correlates Hesse's major works to corresponding periods in his life and his state of mind at those times.

SERRANO, MIGUEL. *C. G. Jung and Hermann Hesse: A Record of Two Friendships.* New York: Schoken Books, 1968. This book, now in paperback, presents intimate insight on the two men from the viewpoint of a member of the Spanish-speaking world, an ambassador from Chile. The photographs are valuable.

ZELLER, BERNHARD. *Portrait of Hesse.* New York: Herder and Herder, 1971. This paperback contains numerous photographs which do not appear in any other biography of Hesse. Its style is refreshing.

ZIOLKOWSKI, THEODORE. *The Novels of Hermann Hesse: A Study in Theme and Structure.* Princeton: Princeton University Press, 1965. This superlative academic study is the best full-length, English-language study of Hesse's work. It is comprehensive, of unusual depth, and thorough in detail, yet it is not heavy or dull reading. Ziolkowski's influence on Hesse scholarship is extensive, many of the original and highly relevant concepts and phrases bearing the unmistakable conciseness which is Ziolkowski's mark.

NOTES

NOTES

NOTES

liffs

Math Review
nd
Verbal Review
or
Standardized Tests

e your time efficiently with exactly the review material you need for standardized tests.

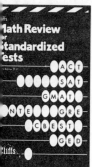

GMAT — SAT — NTE — GRE —
—State Teacher Credential Tests—
PSAT — CBEST — ACT — PPST — GED
and many more!

h Review — 422 pages

Provides insights and strategies for specific problem types, plus intensive review in the most needed basic skills in arithmetic, algebra, geometry and word problems.

Includes hundreds of practice problems to reinforce learning at each step in a unique easy-to-use format.

bal Review — 375 pages

Includes a grammar and usage review, dealing specifically with the concepts that exam-makers consistently use in test questions; exercises reinforce concept understanding at each step.

Extensive practice and strategies in English usage, sentence correction, antonyms, analogies, sentence completion, reading comprehension and timed essay writing.

Cliffs Notes, Inc., P.O. Box 80728, Lincoln, NE 68501

- -

fs Math Review
Standardized Tests $8.95 _____

fs Verbal Review
Standardized Tests $7.95 _____

Cliffs
NOTES

P.O. Box 80728
Lincoln, NE 68501

rice subject to change without notice

ne _____

dress _____

_____ State _____ Zip _____

To understand great authors, you need to read between the lines.

Cliffs Complete Study Editions

The more you learn about the classics, the richer your enjoyment and the deeper your understanding become. These easy-to-use Complete Study editions contain everything a student or teacher needs to study works by Shakespeare or Chaucer. Each illustrated volume includes abundant biographical, historical and literary background information, including a bibliography to aid in selecting additional reading.

The three-column arrangement provides running commentary for the complete Cambridge edition of the Shakespeare plays, plus glossary entries explaining obscu Elizabethan words. The Chaucer titles contain running commentary, individual line of the Middle English text, followed by literal translations in contemporary English and glossaries.

Complete Study Editions
8½ × 11

Shakespeare	Qty.
1416-5 Hamlet	
1419-X Julius Caesar	
1425-4 King Henry IV, Part 1	
1422-X King Lear	
1428-9 Macbeth	
1431-9 Merchant of Venice	
1434-3 Othello	
1438-6 Romeo and Juliet	
1441-6 The Tempest	
1445-9 Twelfth Night	
Chaucer's Canterbury Tales	
1406-8 The Prologue	
1409-2 The Wife of Bath	

Prices subject to change without notice.

$6.95 each

Available at your booksellers, or send this form with your check or money order to **Cliffs Notes, Inc.,** P.O. Box 80728, Lincoln, NE 68501 http://www.cliffs.com

☐ Money order ☐ Check payable to Cliffs Notes, Inc.

☐ Visa ☐ Mastercard Signature_____

Card no. _____ Exp. date_____

Signature _____

Name _____

Address _____

City _____

State _____ Zip_____

Cliffs NOTE